History of
Japan's Intrusions
into Korea

Thirty Images and Documents on *Japan's invasion of Korea*

Edited by Northeast Asian History Foundation

NORTHEAST ASIAN
HISTORY FOUNDATION

Introductory remark

The Joseon dynasty was established in 1392. On October 12, 1897, the dynasty changed its name to the Empire of Korea. On August 29, 1910, Japan forcibly annexed the Empire of Korea and called it Joseon. On August 15, 1945, Joseon was liberated from Japanese colonial rule. For the non-Korean readers who are unfamiliar with this history, the name Korea has been used consistently in this book.

Preface

Koreans commonly refer to Japan as "a country close yet far away." It is because history has continued to drive Korea and Japan apart while their close geographical distance should have made them friendly neighbors. Unfortunately, the bilateral relations of the two countries are now under the gravest circumstances since the establishment of normalization in 1965.

Historical issues are at the root of the strife between Korea and Japan. During the normalization of Korea and Japan in 1965, Japan stayed silent about the historical issues instead of acknowledging and trying to resolve them. Efforts were nevertheless made by both countries to tend to the wounds and bridge the gap. However, the circumstances have recently taken an ill turn as Japan began to prod at historical wounds, and the same circumstances apply to the territorial claims Japan has been making over the Korean island Dokdo.

For Korea and Japan to jointly build peace in the future as close neighbors, they need to confront the wounds of history instead of denying them. To contribute to that cause, the Northeast Asian History Foundation (NAHF) hereby presents *Thirty Images and Documents on Japan's invasion of Korea*, a publication that seeks to accommodate both students and the general public. This book utilizes variety of sources and photographs to arrow what has already been covered through history curricula more accessible and to be considered from new perspectives.

Each of the thirty chapters in this book features a different topic to facilitate a proper understanding of Japan's intrusive activities during its colonial rule over Korea. This book offers an analysis on the excuses and justifications Japan gave such as the "Oriental Peace" for their pillging of the Korean peninsula and points out why Japan's forced occupation of Korea based on an annexation treaty was illegal and unjustifiable. This book also offers descriptions about the projects the Japanese government carried out in Korea such as land surveys, rice production, and cultural rule as well as the laws they established such as the Public Security Preservation Law and the National Mobilization Law. All of these starved Koreans and forced them to make immense sacrifices. This book explains how Japan constantly attempted to brainwash Koreans into believing that they were incapable of gaining independence and ultimately drove them to war in order to annihilate them.

Koreans tend to be well aware of what really happened under Japanese colonial rule. However, certain claims glorifying Japan's past aggressions have recently been circulated, which completely contradict the facts the Koreans have learned and is true. Such distortions and denials of history can do no good to the relations between Korea and Japan.

NAHF has constantly made efforts to spread accurate understandings about Japan's pillaging of Korea and the problems it caused. For a more in-depth exploration of the topics in this book, it may be helpful to read other NAHF publications such as *the Hanil yeoksa jaengjeom: Ilge singmin jibae wa geukbok* [Historical Issues Between Korea and Japan: Overcoming Japanese Colonial Rule], *Ilbon eui asia taepyeongyang jeonjaeng gwa joseonin gangje dongwon* [The Asia-Pacific War and Japan's Forced Mobilization of Koreans], and *Pyeonghwa reul hyanghan geundaejueui haeche: Samil undong baekjunyeon e singminji 'gyeongje seongjang' eul dasi mutda* [Dismantling Modernism for Peace: Reexamining Colonial 'Economic Growth' on the Centennial Anniversary of the March First Independence Movement]. We hope this book can help people form an accurate understanding of how Japan pillaged Korea.

President, Northeast Asian History Foundation

Contents

1

Invasion Under the Pretense of Oriental Peace

Is it true that after the First Sino-Japanese War and the Russo-Japanese War, Japan used "Oriental peace" as an excuse to deprive Korea of its sovereignty? Yes, it is.

Japan disguised their plan to colonize Korea and expand its strength to become the central power of Asia by supporting the Oriental Peace. Japan's idea of Oriental Peace was not intended for each Asian country to equally retain their independence and sovereignty. In 1894, Japan declared the "independence of Korea" and the "preservation of peace in all areas of the Orient" as its purpose in going to war with China. When Japan won the war and signed the Treaty of Shimonoseki with China on April 17, 1895, the treaty's first article stipulated that "China recognizes definitively the full and complete independence and autonomy of Korea." This very article has been introduced in Japanese middle school and high school textbooks. However, the real reason Japan pushed for the independence of Korea was because they wished to pry Korea out of Qing China's grip and place the country under their own command.

Upon the outbreak of the First Sino-Japanese War, the Japanese army seized Gyeongbokgung Palace and mercilessly slaughtered Donghak peasant insurgents of Korea. Since 1894, Korea practically came under the occupation of the Japanese military. On October 8, 1895, dozens of Japanese assassins infiltrated Gyeongbokgung Palace under orders from Miura Goro, the Japanese minister to Korea, and brutally murdered Empress Myeongseong, which has come to be known as the Eulmi Incident.

In February of 1904, Japan went to war with Russia under the pretense of defending Oriental peace and solidifying Korea's independence. The

〈Reference 1〉 The Great Sino-Japanese Battle at Pyongyang (Woodprint, 1894).

Japan allegedly went to war with China for Korea's independence and Oriental peace, but many Koreans fell victim to the war as the Korean peninsula turned into a battlefield and Donghak peasant insurgents were massacred by the Japanese army.

– Source: *Singminji Joseon gwa jeonjaeng misul* [Colonial Korea and Wartime Art] (Seoul: Minjok munje yeonguso, 2004), 17.

Empire of Korea declared that it would maintain neutrality, but Japan forced Korea to enter a treaty on February 23, 1904.

> "For Japan and Korea to maintain an everlasting, unwavering friendship and firmly establish Oriental peace, the Imperial Government of Korea shall place full confidence in the Imperial Government of Japan and accept the advice of the latter in regard to making improvements in administration."
>
> Article 1 of the Korea-Japan Treaty of 1904

While citing friendship and Oriental peace as an excuse, Japan forced Korea into allowing the former to appropriate land anywhere in Korea. Furthermore, Japan plundered resources of the Korean peninsula and mobilized Koreans for war. On August 22, 1904, Japan again forced the Empire of Korea to sign an agreement on appointing foreign advisors, which required the Korean government to retain a Japanese fiscal advisor and a foreign diplomatic advisor that were recommended by the Japanese government. *The Hanil oegugin gomun yongbing e gwanhan hyeobyak* [Korea-Japan Agreement on the Appointment of Foreign Advisors] thereby stripped Korea of its fiscal authority and allowed Japan to interfere in Korea's diplomatic affairs. On February 22, 1905, Japan forcibly incorporated Dokdo, a Korean island into its own territory. Later that year on November 17, Korea was forced to sign a protectorate treaty with Japan that deprived Korea of all diplomatic rights.

The Oriental peace was again used as an excuse in 1910 when Japan forcibly annexed Korea. Japan claimed that the purpose of the annexation was to stop Korea from becoming the source of catastrophe and war because that would be detrimental to Oriental peace.

Among the proponents of Oriental peace at the time were the Korean independence activists such as An Jung-geun and Heo Wi. An Jung-geun suggested that the Oriental countries should be able to enjoy peace and prosperity together. The Oriental peace he envisioned was therefore entirely different from what Japan had in mind.

〈Reference 2〉 An Jung-geun's Vision for Oriental Peace

Once Lushun is opened by Japan, the naval base there should be placed under the joint management of Japan, Qing China, and Korea. Then each country should send a representative to organize and declare the formation of a peace committee. The wisest solution would be for Japan to return Lushun to Qing China and help turn the area into a base for peace.

In terms of securing fiscal resources, the peace committee formed in Lushun should recruit members and collect a membership fee of 1 won from each member. Korea, Qing China, and Japan should jointly establish a bank and issue a currency shared by the three countries so that they may pursue collective economic development. Branches of the bank as well as the peace committee should be installed in the central regions of each country in order to promote fiscal stability.

Young men from Korea, Qing China, and Japan should form a corps and trained to become bilingual so as to encourage them to consider one another as an ally and a brother.

- Quoted from An Jung-geun's meeting with the Chief Justice of the High Court of the Kwantung Government-General on February 17, 1910.

〈Reference 3〉 The Declaration of Korean Revolution by the Uiyeoldan [Righteous Patriots Corps] (Jan 1923)

2. Who Dares to Advocate Administrative Independence, Political Rights, or Autonomy?

Have you forgotten the history of Korea being plundered even before the ink dried on the pledge to preserve Oriental peace and Korea's independence? If administrative independence was achieved without being able to reclaim concessions, how could the people of Korea become anything but starving ghosts? . . . Even if the bandit Japan suddenly transforms into a Buddha or Bodhisattva overnight and dissolves the Japanese Government-General of Korea, returns all the concessions it took, leaves domestic and diplomatic affairs to our discretion, immediately withdraws its troops and police force, instantly summons all Japanese migrants back to their homeland, and leaves us with nominal suzerainty, as long as we remember all of that happened in the past, and as human beings are aware of shame, it would be unthinkable to recognize Japan as Korea's suzerain.

- Source: National Institute of Korean History (History Net).

2

Dokdo, the First Victim of Japan's Territorial Despoliation

During the Russo-Japanese War, Japan declared Dokdo as its territory. Were there justifiable grounds for doing so? Absolutely not, but it was a groundless and unilateral declaration Japan made solely for military purposes. When the Russo-Japanese War erupted, the Imperial Government of Korea declared that it would maintain neutrality. Nevertheless, on February 23, 1904, Japanese troops besieged a palace in Seoul, and the imperial family and government of Korea were coerced into concluding a treaty with Japan. Japan was thereby able to station its armed forces in Korea and appropriate any region on the Korean peninsula for military purposes.

Almost as soon as Japan went to war with Russia, the Japanese army became aware that Ulleungdo and Dokdo were strategically valuable. The two islands were located at an advantageous point where the southbound Vladivostok Fleet of Russia runs into the Combined Fleet of Japan. With the Russian fleet threatening Japan's maritime power in the East Sea, the Japanese Navy lost two of its six warships on May 15, 1904. As such, the Japanese Army was in need of a solution to break through the challenges that they faced; the solution was the installation of watch towers to spy on the movements of enemy warships. On September 1, 1904, the Japanese army installed watch towers on the west and south sides of Ulleungdo. Japan then sent a warship to survey Dokdo for the purpose of installing more watch towers.

On September 25, right before the Japanese army set out to survey Dokdo, a man named Nakai Yozaburo filed a petition for the Japanese government to incorporate Dokdo as its own territory. Nakai had been aware that the island was part of Korean territory and at first tried to apply for a lease through the Japanese government. However, after being encouraged by several Japanese officials including those from the Navy Hydrographic Department, he ultimately filed a petition for the Japanese incorporation of Dokdo. The Japanese Home Ministry was against granting the petition since other countries could suspect it as a Japanese government's attempt to annex Korea. The Foreign Affairs Ministry, on the other hand, was eagerly supportive of the petition as it seemed to be a great opportunity to incorporate Dokdo.

The head of the Foreign Affairs Ministry explained that "installing a watch tower as well as a telegraph and laying a submarine cable at Dokdo would be highly beneficial in surveilling enemy warships." In January 1905, the Russian Baltic Fleet was approaching the Straits of Korea. Under such pressing circumstances, the Japanese government decided to incorporate Dokdo by granting Nakai's petition through a cabinet meeting held on January 28. The remark that "there was no evidence to suggest that the island had been occupied by any other country" indicated that terra nullius had been cited as the grounds for incorporating Dokdo. On February 22, 1905, the governor of Shimane Prefecture officially announced that Dokdo was to be placed under the jurisdiction of Oki Islands.

On July 14, 1905, Japan began installing a watch tower on Dokdo and completed the installation on August 19. A few months later in October and November when the Russo-Japanese war came to an end, submarine cables that connected Ulleungdo, Dokdo, and the city of Matsue in Shimane Prefecture. The military cable linking Jukbyeon, Ulleungdo, Dokdo, and Matsue suggested that Japan's despoliation would eventually reach beyond Dokdo and target the entire Korean peninsula.

Dokdo has historically been part of the Korean territory. Even from a modern legal perspective, the Empire of Korea stipulated its jurisdiction over the island through Imperial Ordinance no. 41 issued on October 25, 1900. Hence, the island was being governed by the Empire of Korea when Japan unilaterally decided to incorporate it as its own territory. Japan's imperialist incorporation of Dokdo signaled the beginning of its plundering of the entire Korean peninsula.

〈Reference 1〉 Arrangement of Watch Tower and Buildings on Dokdo

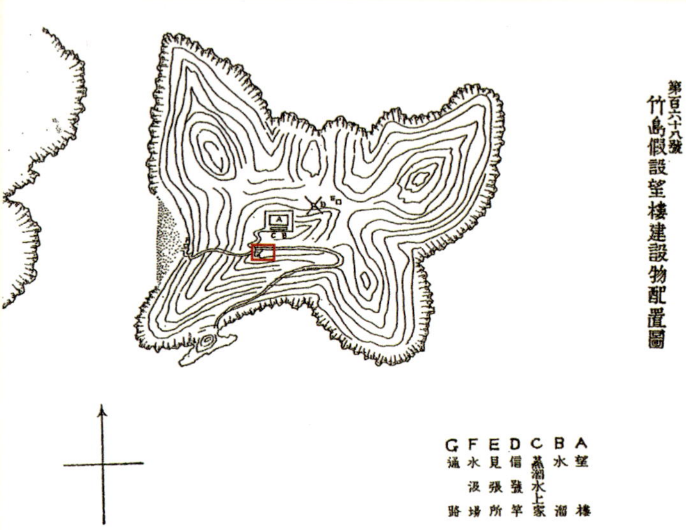

According to this arrangement plan drafted by the Japanese Navy, Building A is the watch tower installed on Dokdo.

- Source: Japan Center for Asian Historical Records.

⟨Reference 2⟩ Announcement of Imperial Ordinance no. 41 (Issued on Oct 25, 1900) in the Official Gazette of the Empire of Korea (Published on Oct 27, 1900)

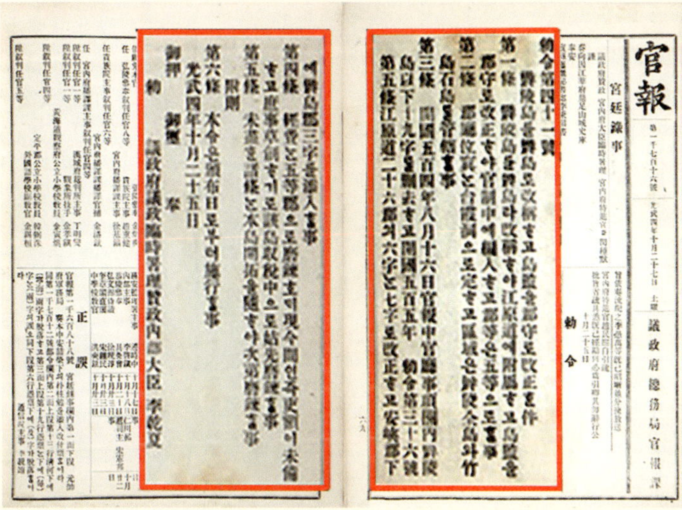

勅令第四十一號

鬱陵島를鬱島로改稱ᄒᆞ고島監을郡守로改正ᄒᆞᆫ件

第一條 鬱陵島를鬱島라改稱ᄒᆞ야江原道에附屬ᄒᆞ고島監을郡守로改正ᄒᆞ야官制中에編入ᄒᆞ고郡等은五等으로ᄒᆞᆯ事

第二條 郡廳位寘ᄂᆞᆫ台霞洞으로定ᄒᆞ고區域은鬱陵全島와竹島石島를管轄ᄒᆞᆯ事

第三條 開國五百四年八月十六日官報中官廳事項欄內鬱陵島以下十九字를刪去ᄒᆞ고開國五百五年勅令第三十六號第五條江原道二十六郡의六字ᄂᆞᆫ七字로改正ᄒᆞ고安峽郡下에鬱島郡三字를添入ᄒᆞᆯ事

第四條 經費ᄂᆞᆫ五等郡으로磨鍊ᄒᆞ되現今間인즉吏額이未備ᄒᆞ고庶事草創ᄒᆞ기로該島收稅中으로姑先磨鍊ᄒᆞᆯ事

第五條 未盡ᄒᆞᆫ諸條ᄂᆞᆫ本島開拓을隨ᄒᆞ야次第磨鍊ᄒᆞᆯ事

附則

第六條 本令은頒布日로부터施行ᄒᆞᆯ事

光武四年十月二十五日

御押 御璽 奉

勅 議政府議政臨時署理贊政內部大臣 李乾夏

※ The announcement is outlined in red.

Translation

Imperial Ordinance no. 41

On the matter of renaming Ulleungdo and Uldo and appointing a governor for the island.

Article 1. Ulleungdo will be renamed as Uldo, designated as a grade 5 county, and ruled by the governor of Gangwon Province.

Article 2. The county office will be located in Taeha-dong and will oversee the whole of Ulleungdo as well as Jukdo and Seokdo.

→ "Seokdo" in the ordinance refers to Dokdo.

- Source: *Digital Ulleung munhwa Daejeon* [Digital Encyclopedia of Ulleung Culture].

3

Armed Resistance Against Japanese Invasion

In Korea, some people valiantly fought against the imperialist Japanese invasion of their land and sovereignty. They are referred to as *uibyeong*, or righteous armies. *Uibyeong* were not official soldiers. They were voluntarily organized militia. In 1907, a British Canadian journalist named Frederick A. McKenzie interviewed uibyeong soldiers and published a book about them. When MckKkenzie asked why they had to engage in a hopeless fight with little chance of winning, a nameless uibyeong soldier replied,

"We will die anyway. That's fine. It's much better to die a free man than to live as a slave of Japan." *Daehan jeguk eui bigeuk* [The Tragedy of the Korean Empire] (Seoul: Jipmoondang, 1999), 190.

Most of the soldiers who fought as *uibyeong* came from ordinary families that had been farming for generations. Yet, they willingly chose to die fighting instead of becoming the slaves of Japan. There were two waves of *uibyeong* resistance near the end of the Korean Empire. The first wave was spurred after an outrage over Japan's murder of Empress Myeongseong in addition to disapproval of forced political reforms. The second wave occurred in response to the Japanese invasion of Korean sovereignty through a series of treaties Korea was coerced into signing with Japan in 1904, 1905, and 1907. The second *uibyeong* resistance tends to be more noteworthy in terms of its organization and activities. While aristocrats and Confucian scholars led *uibyeong* resistances in the beginning, commoners took the lead beyond 1904.

As it went to war with Russia, Japan forced the Korean government into an offensive and defensive alliance through the conclusion of a treaty in February 1904. Once the war was over, Korea was deprived of its diplomatic rights after being forced into another treaty with Japan in November 1905. In 1907, Korea was yet again forced into another treaty with Japan that stripped it of its administrative and judicial power as well as the power to appoint or dismiss government officials. The calamity of the Russo-Japanese War and Japan's repeated invasions of Korean sovereignty caused Confucian scholars and farmers across Korea to form righteous armies against Japan. Upon concluding a seven-article treaty with Korea in 1907, Japan dissolved the Korean Imperial Army to prevent Koreans from resorting to armed resistance in the process of annexing Korea. Some of the soldiers from the former Korean Imperial Army joined righteous armies. The addition of the dissolved soldiers quickly bolstered the fighting power of uibyeong. *Uibyeong* regrouped their forces and prepared to fight the Japanese Army. By the end of 1907, uibyeong soldiers from all thirteen provinces of Korea were reorganized into a combined force. It was the largest and most organized force in the history of *uibyeong*.

Japan resorted to various means to undermine *uibyeong*. While mobilizing Japanese armed forces and military police stationed on the Korean peninsula to carry out direct attacks on *uibyeong*, Japan also employed measures to perturb uibyeong soldiers by persuading them to defect in exchange for exoneration. Countless uibyeong soldiers died in battle or surrendered their weapons from being deceived by the promise of exoneration. Despite the Japanese Army's suppression and placatory measures, a considerable number of *uibyeong* survived and continued to fight. Japan thereby launched an "Operation to Subdue Rioters in the South" in 1909 which involved a large-scale military attack on *uibyeong* in the southwestern region of Korea. The cruel operation cornered *uibyeong* and closed in on them. Under the pursuit of the Japanese Army, uibyeong soldiers fled to coastal areas at first and then to offshore islands, but they were ultimately shot to death. The following quote from *Maecheon yarok* is what a Korean intellectual named Hwang Hyeon wrote after personally witnessing the Japanese suppression of *uibyeong*.

> Uibyeong soldiers dispersed in all directions to save themselves but could not hide. The sturdy charged forward and met their demise in combat while the feeble faced the sword as they tried to crawl their way out. When

they were chased all the way down to Gangjin and Haenam, thousands found themselves with nowhere else to escape and died. (Maecheon yarok, vol. 6, 1909)

To Japan, suppressing *uibyeong* was imperative to depriving Korea of its sovereignty. *Uibyeong* nevertheless fought against Japanese imperialism until their last breath. With the sole purpose of escaping the shackles of a foreign power, helpless, ordinary farmers died as free men at the southern end of the Korean peninsula. Those that survived went abroad to take part in the independence movements.

〈Reference 1〉 Japanese soldiers deployed to suppress *uibyeong*

Frederick A. McKenzie, Shin Bok-ryong trans., *Daehan jeguk eui bigeuk* [The Tragedy of the Korean Empire] (Seoul: Jipmoondang, 1999).

〈**Reference 2**〉 *Joseon pokdo tobeolji*, a record of the Japanese military operation to suppress *uibyeong*.

朝鮮暴徒討伐誌

第一編　暴動ノ起因及經過ノ概要

第一章　暴動ノ起因

其一　舊韓國積年ノ弊政ヨリ來リタル無秩序

火賊ノ跳梁

由來舊韓國政治ノ紊亂其極ニ達シ殊ニ司法行政ノ制度共ニ頽ル弛廢シ草賊野盜ノ類甚タ多ク其火賊ト稱スルモノハ銃器ヲ携ヘ數人乃至數十人集團シテ舊韓國全土隨所ニ横行シ掠奪戕害暴虐ニ意ヲ恣ニセルモ爲政者ハ竟ニ之ヲ裁定スル能ハス而シテ其軍隊ト稱スルモノモ此等火賊ニ比スレハ兵員ノ多寡及武器ノ精否等固ヨリ同日ノ論ニアラスト雖其素質ニ至リテハ殆ント之ト大差ナク地方無賴ノ徒カ單ニ衣食ノ資ヲ得ンカ爲メニ兵營ニ投セルニ過キサルカ故ニ實際兵員ノ多クハ兵器ヲ惡用シ或ハ財貨ヲ强請シ或ハ婦女ヲ姦スル等醜陋ノ行爲ヲ敢テシ寧ロ良民ノ蠹毒タリキ又警察ノ如キモ殆ント單ニ權門暴吏ノ手足トナリ之カ誅

軍隊ノ素質

第一章　暴動ノ起因

—(1)—

4

Coerced into an Illegal Treaty

Japan has maintained their statement that its 1910 annexation and colonial rule of Korea was based on a legitimate treaty. The 1910 Korea-Japan Treaty ws invoid according to the international law. Japan coerced Korea into signing the treaty, which means it was void from the moment it was concluded. Since the late nineteenth century, Japan struggled to revise the unequal treaties it had concluded with other countries including the United States. Meanwhile, it made efforts to secure the grounds that would internationally legitimize its aggression. This was the main reason why Japan carried out its annexation of Korea through a treaty and tried to gain the international society's approval with each step it took. Through the Anglo-Japanese Alliance signed on August 12, 1905 (first established on January 20, 1902) and the Taft-Katsura signed on July 29, 1905, Japan was given the priority to take aggressive actions against Korea. And the peace treaty Japan concluded with Russia on

September 5, 1905 recognized that Korea was under Japan's possession.

Immediately after declaring war against Russia, Japan concluded a treaty with Korea on February 23, 1904 that allowed them to appropriate land at its discretion on the Korean peninsula. On August 22 of the same year, Japan again forced Korea into an agreement on the appointment of foreign advisors, depriving Korea of its fiscal and diplomatic authority. After winning the war against Russia, Japan completely deprived Korea of its diplomatic rights through another treaty concluded on November 17, 1905. When the Japanese government found out that the Korean Emperor Gojong secretly sent emissaries to attend a peace conference at the Hague in order to internationally expose the iniquities of the 1905 Korea-Japan Treaty, Japan forced the emperor into abdication on July 20, 1907. A few days later, Japan deprived Korea of its judicial rights through an additional seven-article treaty concluded on July 24, 1907. On August 1, 1907, Japan dissolved the Korean Imperial Army, and a few years later, forced Korea to surrender its police authority through a memorandum signed on June 24, 1910. Step by step, Japan robbed Korea of its rights, which resulted in Korea surrendering its national rights to Japan through the annexation treaty concluded on August 22, 1910. Meanwhile, Korean insurgents formed righteous armies to counter Japan's aggressions, which Japan did not hesitate to suppress by mobilizing their troops and military police in addition to deploying two army divisions.

To conceal the coercions that could render Japan's treaties with Korea as ineffective according to the international law, Japan attempted to secure legitimacy in terms of the format and procedure through which the treaties were concluded. However, the "consensual" treaties had no formal titles and treaty articles on the delegation of authority were problematic. Japan made it appear as if the treaties had been voluntarily devised by the Korean emperor and the imperial court officials out of their own will, when in reality the Japanese government forced the process using military threat and intimidation. To further obscure the intentions, Japan made conciliatory offers assuring that the status and wealth of the Korean emperor and the imperial court officials would be preserved.

The annexation treaty of 1910 was concluded as a result of Japan's progressive aggression. Hence, it was illegal. Mobilizing armed forces to suppress all those who are against the treaty, from the emperor to the resistant commoners, was an imperialist and wrongful move in every sense of the word.. Article 1 of the treaty stipulates that "His Majesty the Emperor of Korea makes the complete and permanent cession to His Majesty the Emperor of Japan of all rights of sovereignty over the whole of Korea," followed by Article 2 stating that "His Majesty the Emperor of Japan accepts the cession mentioned in the preceding article and consents to the complete annexation of Korea to the Empire of Japan."

Nevertheless, on April 26, 1926, Emperor Sunjong of Korea on his death bed, to Jo Jeong-gu, the head of the Department of the Royal Household Department, that he would never sign a treaty with articles which demanded him to surrender his kingdom (Jul 8, 1926 edition of the daily newspaper *Sinhan Ilbo*).

〈Reference 1〉 Lampoon of the Forcibly Concluded 1905 Korea-Japan Treaty in Korean Newspaper (Publisher: Homer Hulbert)

Despite being threatened by Japanese soldiers, the Emperor of Korea indignantly refused to sign the treaty, but it five traitors conspired against the Emperor and concluded the treaty without consent. A satirical twist is made on the cartoon's title at the lower right corner by replacing one of the characters with a homonymic character that means "threaten" (脅) instead of "cooperate" (協).

- Source: National Institute of Korean History (History Net).

〈Reference 2〉 Japanese Soldiers Demanding Emperor Gojong's Abdication

Japanese soldiers in an armed protest for Emperor Gojong's abdication at Gyeongungung Palace in 1906

- Source: Gang Man-gil, 20 *segi uri yeoksa* [Twentieth Century Korean History] (Seoul: Changbi, 2018), 31.

〈Reference 3〉 Comparison of Annexation Treaty Protocols

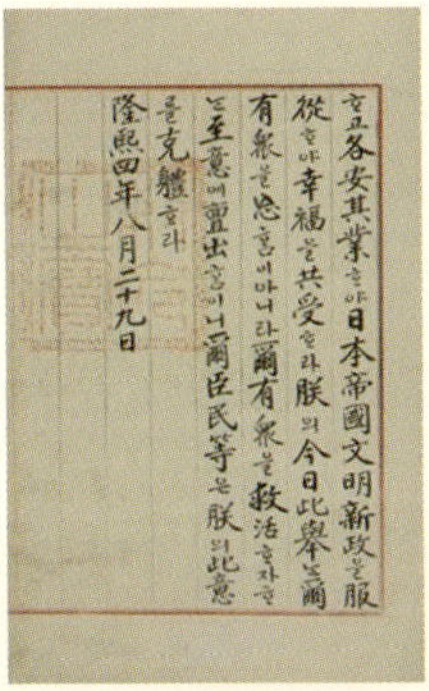

하고各安其業하야日本帝國文明新政을服
從하야幸福을共受하라朕의今日此擧는爾
有衆을忘함이아니라爾有衆을救活하자하
는至意에出함이니爾臣民等은朕의此意
를克體하라
隆熙四年八月二十九日

Emperor Sunjong's Mandate

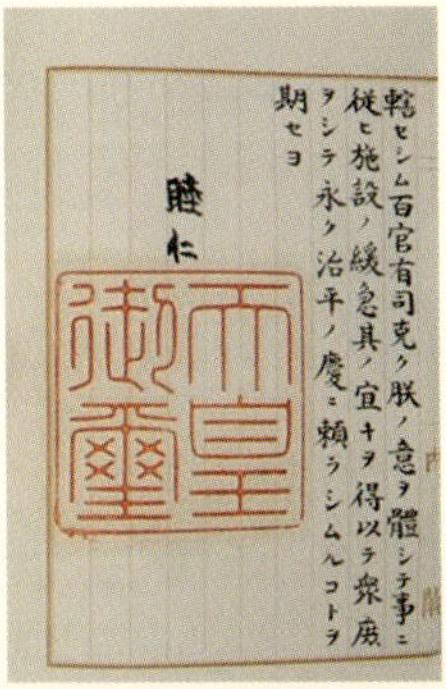

輯セシム百官有司克ク朕ノ意ヲ體シテ事ニ
從ヒ施設ノ緩急其ノ宜キヲ得以テ衆庶
ヲシテ永ク治平ノ慶ニ頼ラシムルコトヲ
期セヨ
睦仁
天皇御璽

Japanese Protocol of the Annexation Treaty

While the Japanese protocol of the Korea-Japan Annexation Treaty (right) bears the state seal of Japan (天皇御璽) and Japanese emperor's signature Mutsuhito (睦仁), the mandate the Korean Emperor Sunjong proclaimed bears the royal seal (勅命之寶) instead of the state seal of Korea without the Korean emperor's signature Yi Cheok (李拓).

- Source: Yi Tae-jin and Rhee Sang-chan, *Joyak euro bon hanguk byeonghap* [The Annexation of Korea Through Treaties] (Seoul: Northeast Asian History Foundation, 2010), 282, 287.

5

Annexation for the Happiness of Koreans?

"His Majesty the Emperor of Japan and His Majesty the Emperor of Korea, having in view the especially close relations between their respective countries, desiring to promote the mutual happiness of the two nations and assure permanent Oriental peace, and being convinced that these objectives can be best attained by the annexation of Korea to the Empire of Japan, have resolved to conclude a treaty of such annexation. . ."

- Preamble of the Korea-Japan Annexation Treaty (Aug 22, 1910)

"For nearly four years, my government earnestly attempted to improve government administration in Korea and managed to make noteworthy progress, but Korea's current system remains insufficient to maintain perfect public order and considerable doubt over the system has failed to put the people within its boundaries at ease, so in order to maintain public stability and promote public welfare. . ."

-Emperor Meiji's Message Regarding the Korea-Japan Annexation Treaty (Aug 29, 1910)

The terms "Happiness" (of Koreans), "prosperity" (of Korea), and "Oriental peace" commonly appeared in treaties Korea signed with Japan in 1904, *Eulsaneukyak* of 1905, and Annexation Treaty of 1910. These expressions were a pretext for neglecting independence of the Korean Empire and taking away their diplomatic rights and sovereignty. Hence, the words happiness and peace were no more than a means for Japan to hide its intention to pillage the Korean peninsula. The rationale that Japan annexed Korea and exercised colonial rule over them was based on the notion that Koreans were barbaric and remained a static society. According to Japan's logic, the "passive" and "uncivilized" Koreans and their society were in need of instructions from an advanced country that successfully civilized through modernization, like Japan.

Japan's despoliation of Korea also had to do with its narrow, nationalist perception of history. In other words, Korea had remained as a vassal of China whereas Japan had maintained its independence as a divine nation ruled by kings from the same lineage since antiquity. This distorted view further developed after the Meiji Restoration in 1868. Such assertions developed into the rationale that a divine nation like Japan should rule over its neighbor Korea for the country's happiness.

Visible progress in administration had to be shown to secure legitimacy for Japanese colonial rule which allegedly aimed at administrative improvement and public welfare of Korea. The Japanese Government-General of Korea publicized the contributions the colonial rule made to Korea's economic development through publications like Sijeong 30 nyeonsa [Thirty Years of Colonial Rule] and held events to celebrate certain anniversaries of Japanese colonial rule such as the 1915 Joseon Industrial Fair and the 1929 Joseon Exhibition. Nevertheless, Koreans were not deceived by the justifications Japan made, hence the declaration of independence for Korea was claimed on February 8, 1919.

Being ruled by Japan was humiliating and mortifying for the people of Korea. When Korea lost its diplomatic rights, Min Yeong-hwan* laid bare the humiliation Japan caused to his country and compatriots before taking his own life. Bak Eun-sik** expressed the grief of losing national sovereignty by replacing one of the characters in his 1915 book Hanguk tongsa [The Painful History of Korea] with a homonymic character that means "painful" (痛) instead of "general" (通). There was no happiness for Koreans who had lost their country.

* Young hwan Min (1861~1905) was a minister of the Korean Empire. On November 17, 1905 he ended his own life as an act of resistance against the Eulsa Treaty Japan imposed on Korea to deprived Korea of its diplomatic sovereignty.

** Eun-sik Park(1859~1925) was a patriotic scholar who worked as an independence activist. He wrote 「Hwangseong Shinmun」 and 「Daehan Maeil Shinbo」, criticizing the Japanese imperial aggression in support of the independence movements. After the deprivation of Korea's autonomy in 1910, while working mainly in China, he wrote books such as 「The History of Korea」 and 「The History of the Korean Independence Movement」, to help raise national pride and identity.

〈Reference 1〉 February 8 Declaration of Independence (1919)

Contrary to what was declared upon annexation, the policies Japan adopted for the rule of Korea neglected the happiness and interests of our people, executed inhumane policies by taking away our people's right to vote, their freedom of assembly, association, and speech, and even inhibiting freedom of religion and business. All agencies involved in administration, jurisdiction, and law enforcement have violated the human rights of the Koreans... As such, our people are bound to suffer damage since their interests run counter to those of the Japanese in every respect, which is why our people fight for independence for the sake of their right to survive.

- Source: Declaration of Independence (Feb 8, 1919).

〈Reference 2〉 Min Yeong-hwan's Final Words (1919)

The country's humiliation and the disgrace brought upon to its people will devastate Koreans in the upcoming competition for survival. How can you gentlemen not know that those who seek life shall die and that those who seek death shall live? Through his death, Yeong-hwan sought to repay the emperor's kindness and apologize to his twenty million compatriots. Though Yeong-hwan will be gone, he vows to assist you from beyond his grave, so if his compatriots can manage to regain their freedom and independence by keep fighting and working together in solidarity, the deceased shall smile with joy in the dark otherworld. Alas, let us not be the least bit discouraged. I bid my twenty million compatriots farewell.

- Source: *Daehan maeil sinbo* (Dec 1, 1905).

※ The daily newspaper *Daehan maeil sinbo* published the final words Min Yeong-hwan left on his card shortly before killing himself on November 30 out of despair over the treaty concluded with Japan on November 17, 1905.

〈Reference 3〉 *Hanguk tongsa* by Bak Eun-sik (1915)

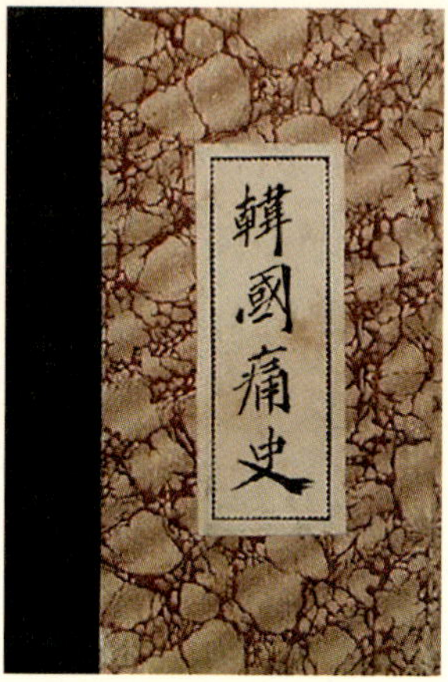

- Source: National Institute of Korean History (History Net).

6

Japanese Propaganda of its Imperialist Policies

After depriving Korea of its sovereignty in 1910, Japan engaged in a propaganda to justify its invasion and colonial rule of Korea. The propaganda, was established as early as 1875 when the Japanese warship Un'yō trespassed into the waters near Ganghwa Island and attacked Korean guards. The Japanese Foreign Minister Terashima Munenori ordered Japanese diplomats stationed in the West to publicize that the reason Japan involved a warship and envoys was to expand trade with Korea and ensure that they don't attack ships like the Un'yō coming ashore in search of supplies.

Propaganda through diplomatic channels gradually branched out to civilian channels. The Japanese government sought to propagandize through journalists or English newspapers distributed in the neighborhoods of foreign residents in Korea. An example of this would be the role J. A. Cockerill played when Empress Myeongseong was assassinated in 1895. As a correspondent of the New York Herald, Cockerill was in Seoul at the time, collecting information from Horace N. Allen, the United States Consul General of Korea, and Karl I. Weber, the Russian Consul General of Korea, while remaining in close contact with Inoue Kaoru, a Japanese special ambassador in Seoul at the time. Cockerill's article in the December 5, 1895 edition of the New York Herald solely represented Japan's side of the story.

DETERMINED TO DO JUSTICE

...The Count wished to know whether the arrest of ex-Minister Miura and thirty-six of the Japanese conspirators upon their arrival in Japan did not have a reassuring effect in foreign circles in seoul. I informed him that this act changed the entire tone of the foreign legations, being as it was, an earnest of determination of the Japanese government to not only repudiate and execrate the bloody performance of October 8, but to hunt down and punish its nationals who were largely responsible for it. ...and he was determined to do whatever was in his power to convince mankind that his government thoroughly abhorred and repudiated the shameful deed. ...

(John A. Cockerill, Count Inouye Talks On Corea. Japan's special ambassador to the hermit kingdom states his views to Colonel Cockerill. Full justice to be done, New York Herald, Dec. 5, 1895)

Through his article, Cockerill underlined Inoue's concern of how foreign powers might react to the "barbaric act" and the Japanese government's "determination to do justice" in the assassination of the Korean empress arranged by a Japanese ex-minister. Cockerill's description gave the illusion that Japan's occupation of Korea was necessary to guarantee "permanent peace" for Korea, showing that Japan had sought to justify its imperialist invasions through a foreign journalist.

After its annexation of Korea in 1910, Japan temporarily eased up on the international propaganda until the need for it resurfaced because of the March First Independence Movement in 1919. Japan's military suppression of the movement garnered international interest for exposing the barbaric reality of Japanese colonial rule. Christian missionaries in Korea contributed to drawing attention to Korea's situation, and so did the movements that took place overseas for Korea's independence. In Philadelphia, Seo Jae-pil established the Bureau of Information for the Republic of Korea in April 1919. The Bureau was formed in resistance against Japanese propaganda declaring that Japan's rule over Korea was exemplary and that Korea was incapable to be independency governes. Seo Jae-pil also acquired the monthly magazine Freedom and Peace published by the Korean Student League of America and changed its name to Korea Review. Korea Review aimed to inform the American society about the March First Independence Movement in Korea, developments in independence movements outside Korea, and criticisms about the Japanese colonial rule.

To stop Koreans overseas from exposing the truthbehind of its colonial rule, Japan expanded its policy on international propaganda. In December 1920, the Japanese Government-General of Korea launched the Korea

〈Reference 1〉 *Freedom and Peace and Korea Review*

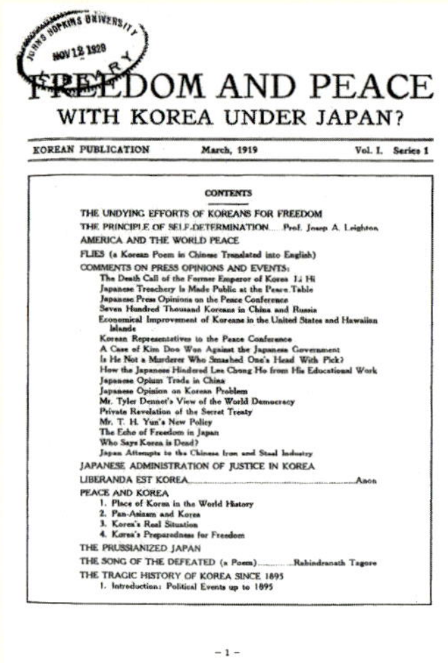

FREEDOM AND PEACE
WITH KOREA UNDER JAPAN?

KOREAN PUBLICATION　March, 1919　Vol. I. Series 1

CONTENTS

THE UNDYING EFFORTS OF KOREANS FOR FREEDOM
THE PRINCIPLE OF SELF-DETERMINATION ...... Prof. Josep A. Leighton
AMERICA AND THE WORLD PEACE
FLIES (a Korean Poem in Chinese Translated into English)
COMMENTS ON PRESS OPINIONS AND EVENTS:
The Death Call of the Former Emperor of Korea Li Hi
Japanese Treachery Is Made Public at the Peace Table
Japanese Press Opinions on the Peace Conference
Seven Hundred Thousand Koreans in China and Russia
Economical Improvement of Koreans in the United States and Hawaiian Islands
Korean Representatives to the Peace Conference
A Case of Kim Doo Won Against the Japanese Government
Is He Not a Murderer Who Smashed One's Head With Pick?
How the Japanese Hindered Lee Chong Ho from His Educational Work
Japanese Opium Trade in China
Japanese Opinion on Korean Problem
Mr. Tyler Dennet's View of the World Democracy
Private Revelation of the Secret Treaty
Mr. T. H. Yun's New Policy
The Echo of Freedom in Japan
Who Says Korea is Dead?
Japan Attempts to the Chinese Iron and Steel Industry
JAPANESE ADMINISTRATION OF JUSTICE IN KOREA
LIBERANDA EST KOREA ...... Anon
PEACE AND KOREA
1. Place of Korea in the World History
2. Pan-Asiasm and Korea
3. Korea's Real Situation
4. Korea's Preparedness for Freedom
THE PRUSSIANIZED JAPAN
THE SONG OF THE DEFEATED (a Poem) ...... Rabindranath Tagore
THE TRAGIC HISTORY OF KOREA SINCE 1895
1. Introduction: Political Events up to 1895

– 1 –

KOREA REVIEW
(Application for entry as second-class mail in Philadelphia Post Office)

Price 20 Cents　JUNE, 1919　Vol. I., No. 4

A Monthly Journal devoted to the
Cause of
Political and Religious
Freedom for Korea

Published by
THE KOREAN STUDENTS LEAGUE OF AMERICA
Under the auspices of the
BUREAU OF INFORMATION FOR THE REPUBLIC OF KOREA
[illegible] CHESTNUT STREET, PHILADELPHIA, PA.

– 33 –

Information Committee aimed at internally and externally clarifying the reality of colonial rule and informed about the meticulousness of policies for colonial rule. As such, the Committee was responsible for producing materials such as magazines, booklets, and films to be utilized in international propaganda activities. For propaganda targeting the West, the Government-General took advantage of Christianity. The following recollection by Moriya Eifu, a Government-General official who was involved in producing propaganda materials, fully revealed what the Japanese government sought to achieve through these activities.

> We went to great pains to thwart propaganda in various countries, especially counter-propaganda in the United States about the Government-General's rule over Korea. ... We decided to begin by sending someone suited for the purpose to a target area and Mr. Yamamoto Tadayoshi became the first to be sent to the United States. Mr. Yamamoto was a pastor of the Japanese Congregational Church. Whereas sending a specialist carries the potential of causing a misunderstanding, we believed a pastor of a congregational church like Mr. Yamamoto would not raise concern among the Americans. So, we suggested for him disguise his intention he had come to experience the christian culture in America, when his actual intention was to inform Americans about the reality of the Government-General's new policies. Chōsen gyōsei henshūkyoku ed., *Chōsen tōchi hiwa* [Unknown Episodes in Japan's Rule of Korea] (Tokyo: Teikoku chihō gyōsei gakkai, 1937).

The "counter-propaganda about the Government-General's rule over Korea" from above refers to the overseas activities of Korean independence activists. The case Moriya mentions in the passage suggests that the Government-General made active use of civilKorians for international propaganda, such as a pastor of the Japan Congregational Church, and preferred to manipulate them from behind the scenes. Japan invested more serious efforts to carry out international propaganda beyond the Mukden Incident in 1931.

7

The Survey to Seize Land

Immediately after annexing Korea in 1910, Japan conducted a land survey on the Korean peninsula. The survey was publicized as an opportunity to establish modern ownership of land in Korea. Was that indeed the reason why Japan launched the survey?

The Empire of Korea originally limited foreigners from owning or trading land within its territory. It was to prevent wearing foreigners plundering the land resources. The Japanese Residency-General of Korea dismissed the limitation and promulgated Edict No. 66 "Rules on the Certification of Lands and Houses" on October 26, 1906, which allowed foreigners to own land in Korea. In 1908, Edict No. 47 "Rules on the Certification of Land or House Ownership" was promulgated to establish a procedure to certify changes and safeguard ownership of land. Thus, Such measures legalized the ownership and trade of land by foreigners in the Empire of Korea.

In 1912, the Japanese Government-General of Korea promulgated the "Ordinance on the Certification of Real Estate in Joseon" and the "Ordinance on the Registration of Real Estate in Joseon." These ordinances created an institutional foundation for wholly recognizing the rights of foreigners, especially the Japanese, to own and trade land in Korea. Ultimately, there were measures Japan took to gain control over Korea while helping their people migrate and settle down in Korea. For that same purpose, the existing land measurement system of Korea based on yield proved to be a hindrance, making it necessary for Japan to conduct a land survey ahead of tailoring the system to its advantage.

In September 1910, soon after Korea became annexed, the Government-General created a temporary bureau to prepare for land surveying, and once the land survey ordinance was promulgated in 1912, a nationwide survey was launched. The survey had two main goals. One was to determine the owner of each land, which secured a list of people who paid the land tax for the Government General. Land ownership was to be confirmed according to the principle of reporting, which required the owner to report the details of their land ownership in order to receive official confirmation. Each district was responsible for reporting the state-owned land within their jurisdiction. The lands owned by the Korean imperial family or government as well as public lands of ambiguous ownership were classified as state-owned land and fell under the possession of the Government-General. The Second goal was to clarify land prices. The price of land was used as the standard for levying tax, so the Government-General hoped to ensure a stable inflow of tax revenue through the land survey. Sure enough, land tax revenue rose 159 percent in the span of a decade. During the land survey, an exponential increase in taxable land occurred, but not because more farmland had been cultivated. Rather, it was because lands that were previously left out of the register became included, resulting in an increase of taxable land. The land survey therefore allowed Japan to collect enough tax revenue to finance its colonial rule over Korea instead of having to channel funds from mainland Japan.

As their ownership of land became legally ensured, Japan steadily plundered the land resources of Korea, which led to an increase in their land ownership. On the contrary, land ownership turned into an increasingly remote possibility for Korean farmers. At the time Korea was annexed, middle-class farmers occupied 60.7 percent of the Korean farming population, but that percentage dropped to 42.7 in 1932. The percentage of tenant farmers, on the other hand, jumped from 36.8 to 54.2 percent over the same time period. These changes represent how Japan was able to build a stable foundation for its colonial rule of Korea.

〈Reference 1〉 Rise in Japanese Land Ownership in Korea

(Unit: 1 *jeongbo* = 9,917.4㎡)

Year	Total Area of Farmland	State-owned Farmland (Owned by the Government-General)	Japanese Ownership	Farmland Owned by the Oriental Development Company
1910	2,464,903	97,460	69,312	10,944
1911	2,705,216		93,380	25,265
1912	2,846,935		107,980	44,549
1913	2,885,911	-	155,862	60,529
1914	2,959,503		159,861	65,395
1915	3,107,605		169,007	68,674
1916	3,589,503	124,499	236,586	68,671
1917	3,875,080		-	69,550
1918	4,342,090		-	69,446
1919	4,324,678		-	70,554

- Source: Statistical Yearbook of the Japanese Government-General of Korea.

〈Reference 2〉 The Japanese Survey of Korean Land

Japan placed Seoul at the center of its nationwide survey of Korean land. The survey disregarded the existing land measurement system and arbitrarily adopted Japanese methods instead. The photos show an altitude reference being measured in Seoul (above) and triangulation being performed in different area (below).

- Source: Japanese Government-General of Korea, *Joseon toji josa saeop bogoseo* [Report on the Land Survey of Joseon] (1918).

8

Japanese Invasion and The Gongchangje System

Some argue that the Japanese military "comfort women" were not victims of the war, but part of a system of legalized brothels at the time referred to as *gongchangje*(公娼制). What was *gongchangje* and why did Japan introduce it to colonial Korea? *Yugwak*(遊廓), which refers to licensed quarters in Korea, is a term that originated from the Japanese language. In Japan, *gongchangje* first emerged in Edo during the early seventeenth century and then became "modernized" after the Meiji Restoration. To keep soldiers and urban laborers committed to achieving national prosperity and bolster military morale, the Japanese government believed state-controlled prostitution was essential in providing the "comfort" they required and protecting them from sexually transmitted diseases. Through a couple of revisions made since 1873, the framework of *gongchangje* became specified, requiring prostitutes to be registered, reside within a designated area, be regularly tested for sexually transmitted diseases, and pay taxes. The police were entrusted with the management of prostitutes. The Japanese government publicized that prostitutes were "free agents" under the *gongchangje* system, but in reality, women were not acknowledged as contracting entities. Japanese culture was based on a patriarchal family system in which the male head was recognized as the family representative, meaning a prostitute could only exercise her legal rights with the approval of the male head of her family.

As Japan invaded the Korean peninsula, the Japanese pimps followed government officials and troops to Korea and opened business with the prostitutes they had brought along from their homeland. The Japanese government acquiesced the operation of these businesses, thinking that it would be helpful to colonizing Korea, and even began to manage prostitution in order to protect its troops as well as Japanese colonizers from sexually transmitted diseases. Since the 1880s, legalized brothels began to operate around Korea ports opened by the Japanese and then settled down as a system in 1916 when the Japanese military created divisions to be stationed in Korea. In areas like Gyeongseong (Seoul) or Hamgyeong Province where Japanese troops were concentrated, prostitutes, hostesses, and entertainers were more strictly tested for sexually transmitted diseases. In the 1910s when Korea was under the military rule of Japan, prostitution was managed by the Japanese military police. The laws and regulations that legalized brothels in Korea in 1916 basically imitated those established in Japan in 1900. The difference was that while prostitutes had to be above eighteen years old in Japan, they could be seventeen in Korea. Compared to Japan, the system in colonial

Korea therefore prioritized the interests of brothels rather than the rights of prostitutes.

Through the aforementioned process, brothels became legalized in colonial Korea which led to the formation of a human trafficking. They were criticized for such practices throughout the colonial period. Brokers were often referred to as "human flesh dealers" or "kidnapping demons." Nevertheless, the police indiscriminately issued business permits to employment brokers, which caused people to lament that "it is difficult to understand how permission can be given to such corrupt practices" (Nov 9, 1924 edition of *Choson Ilbo*). Brokers fabricated family registers in order to act as a proxy in signing prostitution contracts and used loans made to prostitutes as leverage to chain women to prostitution. Hence, the process through which women were turned into prostitutes was no different from human trafficking, causing them to live like slaves in licensed quarters.

After entering into national mobilization mode in 1938, the Government-General cited emergency circumstances as an excuse to force businesses such as restaurants, cafés, and bars to either shut down or switch to a different category of business. Legalized brothels, however, were an exception. When the Second Sino-Japanese War broke out, licensed quarters' revenue increased as Japanese soldiers invoided through Korea. The Government-General facilitated the soldiers' use of licensed quarters by tightening its control over the quarters and strictly testing prostitutes for sexually transmitted diseases. After the war, the comfort women system was actively developed and the licensed quarters already under government control became utilized as comfort stations for the Japanese military.

〈Reference 1〉

The daily newspaper *Sidae Ilbo* published a six-installment article titled "Human Flesh Market" which criticized human trafficking under the legalized brothel system.

- Source: *Sidae Ilbo*, August 24, 26, 28, 1925.

9

Cultural Rule Aimed at National Divide

After the March First Independence Movement, Japan advertised its adoption of a cultural approach to colonial administration as the "cultural rule." Did Japan's mode of colonial rule actually change? Unfortunately not. The word "cultural" had been introduced to evade the fierce acts of resistance that the people of Korea carried out against Japan's military rule in the 1910s such as the March First Independence Movement. It was part of a sophisticated ploy aimed at creating a divide among the people of Korea.

After the March First Independence Movement, Saitō Makoto became appointed as the Japanese Governor-General of Korea. The purpose of his appointment was to send a non-military official to serve as the Governer-General in the hopes of undermining the people of Korea's urge to resist during the March First Independence Movement. Saitō was, however, non-military in name only. He was a civilian at the time of his appointment only because he had retired from the Japanese Navy where he once served as an admiral and Minister of the Navy. Upon Saitō's arrival at Gyeongseong Station, a bomb was thrown at him by the Korean activist Gang U-gyu, an incident that most likely left an indelible impression on Saitō as to how desperately Koreans desired their independence.

To comfort the public after the March First Independence Movement, Governor-General Saitō replaced military rule with cultural rule. On the surface, cultural rule advocated ① government reform through the elimination of bureaucracy and administrative formalities, ② abolition of ethnic discrimination by hiring Korean citizens as officials and offering them better treatment, ③ promotion of popular will by granting the freedom of speech, publication, and assembly, ④ improvement of public welfare by making institutional improvements to education, industry, transportation, law enforcement, and hygiene, ⑤ fostering folk customs and civil power through an autonomous local government system, and ⑥ respect for the cultures and customs of Korea. The alleged purpose of the cultural rule was to abolish ethnic discrimination, encourage Korean citizens to express their opinion, and promote cultural and industrial development.

As a demonstration of the cultural rule, the military force of the 1910s was replaced with an ordinary police system. The replacement was, however, a superficial measure that actually resulted in a significant increase in the size of the police force under the cultural rule. The number of police stations surged more than threefold over a single year from 751 prior to 1919 to 2,716 in 1920, and the number of policemen tripled from 5,400 in 1918 to 18,000 in 1920. As a result, even though an ordinary police system was being operated, the police were reinforced to suppress both ordinary civilians and nationalistic movements in Korea. After experiencing the March First Independence Movement, the Government-General of Korea also made efforts to publicize the achievements from a decade of colonial rule to overturn the negative public opinion that was formed in the West towards Japan's aggressive colonial suppression and persecution of missionaries. The Government-General further sought to propagandize that Korea was incapable of autonomy in order to emphasize the futility of activities such as the March First Independence Movement.

Above all, Saitō's cultural policy aimed at increasing the number of pro-Japanese Koreans, which was stipulated in his *Plan Regarding the People of Korea*. The Government-General of Korea cultivated and broadly utilized many pro-Japanese Koreans "willing to risk their lives" to help build pro-Japanese public opinions, form pro-Japanese groups, uncover and collect information on independence activists, and win them over. Organizations like *Gyopunghoe* [Society for Moral Correction], *Gungmin hyeophoe* [Citizens' Society], and *Daedong dongjihoe* [Comrades of Greater East Asia] were formed to promote pro-Japanese views among the public. Prominent landowners or capitalists formed pro-Japanese groups such as the *Daejeong chinmokoe* [Grand Society of Industrialists] and *Yuminhoe* [People's Aid Association] while Confucian scholars formed pro-Japanese groups like the *Daedong samunhoe* [Great Eastern Confucian Society] and *Yudo jinheunghoe* [Society to Promote

Confucianism]. A government-controlled group called *Joseon sojakhoe sangjohoe* [Aid Society for Joseon Tenant Farmers] was also formed by peasant farmers to undermine the nationalistic movements. Under the pretext of promoting popular will, some bourgeois nationalist activities were permitted and absorbed into the framework of colonial rule. The disputes surrounding tenant farming and labor issues were used as an excuse to assure middle class landowners and capitalists of their status and to turn them into pro-Japanese collaborators. Meanwhile, groups that were against colonial rule were thoroughly oppressed by the police through the Public Security Preservation Law. The Government-General's cultural rule was therefore a policy aimed to create division among Koreans and undermine Korean activists involved in nationalist movements.

〈Reference 1〉

Second from the left is Ugaki Kazushige (宇垣一成), the sixth Japanese Governor-General of Korea, and to his right is Saitō Makoto, the third and fifth Japanese Governor-General of Korea.

- Source: National Institute of Korean History (History Net).

〈Reference 2〉 Plan Regarding the People of Joseon (Excerpt)

① The Need for Pro-Japanese Organizations: A central pro-Japanese figure needs to be found among Korean citizens, someone who shares our ideals and spirit and is willing to devote their lives for them. That figure can be instructed to motivate people from different classes and backgrounds including nobles, aristocrats, Confucian scholars, millionaires, entrepreneurs, teachers, and religious workers to form various pro-Japanese organizations, for which the aforementioned central figure will afterwards be rewarded with considerable conveniences and aid to be able to remain sufficiently active.

② Religious social movements

③ Cultivating Talent: Civilian community leaders and henchmen can be given considerable aid to cultivate pro-Japanese figures in Korea under the excuse of offering education to cultivate talented intellectuals.

④ Aiding the educated: Unproductive aristocrats and Confucian scholars leading an idle life with no fixed occupation can be encouraged to find ways to make a living and be steered (toward the pro-Japanese path).

⑤ Affiliating with capitalists: People in Korea can be warned of the propensities of relationships between capitalists and laborers or landowners and tenants that are likely to emerge in the future, while people in the mainland (Japan) can be persuaded to believe that developing Korea and resolving issues there desperately require partnerships with mainland capitalists.

⑥ Rural instruction: Considerable conveniences and aid can be provided to civilian community leaders for them to make efforts in instructing rural Korea ... All sorts of conveniences such as granting some state-owned forest land or profiting from it would be made available under the authorities' consent.

⑦ Establishing and using a propaganda agency: Another solution could be to establish a secret propaganda agency that utilizes idle folk for verbal or written propaganda and thereby scare and surprise seditious Korean citizens.

The aforementioned methods can be used to distinguish between pro- and anti-Japanese so that the actions of the anti-Japanese can be directly or indirectly restricted while conveniences and aid can be offered, within permissible circumstances, to the pro-Japanese.

- Source: Japanese Government-General of Korea, *Saitō Makoto Papers*, 9; National Institute of Korean History (History Net).

10

Political Discrimination Amid Deceptive Slogans

Were the people of Korea and Japan politically equal under Japan's colonial rule of Korea? Japan promoted the slogan "*ilsi dongin*"(一視同仁), which meant that everyone would be treated equally without discrimination, but in reality, Japan never gave much thought to the equality of its people and those of Korea. On the surface, Japan's colonial policies aimed for equality among Japan and Korea to eventually turn Korea into a region that belonged to Japan like Honshu, Shikoku, or Kyushu. In order to do so, they had to eliminate the gap in living standards that existed between Korea and Japan. This was why Japan carried out a policy of assimilation, assuming that equalizing living standards would turn Koreans into members of the same civilization as the Japanese, subject to the same institutions and laws administered by the Japanese emperor.

Japan nevertheless continued to discriminate Korea throughout its colonial rule. The rationale was that because the gap between the living standards was considerable, it was necessary to first bring barbaric and inferior Korea up to par with Japan. All the discriminating laws and system Japan introduced to Korea were based on the same rationale. For instance, the school system was arranged differently from Japan according to the Korea Educational Ordinance. The Ordinance on Colleges was not even implemented because establishing colleges in Korea was deemed impossible. Yet, what was deemed necessary for colonial rule, laws and systems were implemented almost at the same time as in Japan. For instance, the Public Security Preservation Law established in Japan in 1925 immediately went into effect in Korea. The law's purpose in Japan was to suppress socialist movements, but in Korea, it was used to suppress independence movements. Either Security Regulations or the Security Law could be applied to political associations and assemblies, but the people of Korea were mostly subjected to the Security Law and thus suffered harsher punishments than the Japanese people.

Discrimination based on the differences in living standards equally applied to various political activities. When the Government-General was established in 1910, some Korean citizens were allowed to take part in politics. Pro-Japanese figures were appointed as members of an advisory council called *Jungchuwon* created within the Government-General. Unlike its grand name, though, the council had no authority. After the March First Independence Movement, "promotion of popular will" surfaced as a catchphrase under Japan's cultural rule. Circulation was permitted to some newspapers (*Chosun Ilbo*, *Dong-a Ilbo*) and magazines

(*Changjo*, *Pyeheo*, Baekjo) published by Korean citizens and there were rumors that voting rights or autonomy might be granted to the people of Korea. Such rumors were enticing enough to trigger a certain degree of disintegration in some independence movements, but the rumors were never proven to be true until the fall of Imperial Japan.

Under Japanese colonial rule, there were two ways Korean citizens could gain the right to vote. One was to form an independent assembly in Korea and the other was to have a Korean representative take part in the Imperial Diet of Japan. When the talk of these two options within the Government-General became disclosed, some in the pro-Japanese faction responded by launching a campaign for voting rights. However, public antagonism towards the campaign was strong enough to result in the murder of Min Won-sik, the governor of Goyang who led the campaign. Some of the Korean bourgeoisie (right-wing nationalists), on the other hand, began to call for autonomy. This call for autonomy was, however, based on an approach that strayed from the complete independence of Korea. The nationalist camp in Korea thereafter split into compromising and non-compromising nationalists.

Regardless, the Government-General had no intention of granting autonomy or allowing campaigns for it. It only permitted a distorted, partial form of local autonomy based on the idea of promoting popular will. Advisory councils were created for schools as well as the administrative units of *bu*, *myeon*, and do (*unit*, *county*, *and province*) through the partial reform of local administrative systems and this was advertised as part of a training for local autonomy in Korea. Among the advisory councils, only 24 of them were formed through an election at *myeons* where there were many Japanese residents or Korean landowners while the rest were formed through the appointment of their respective governors. Provincial advisory councils were also formed through governor appointments. As for the school advisory councils, members representing a *bu* were appointed through election while those representing a *myeon* were appointed by the governor. Furthermore, voting rights were limited to those in a bu or myeon who paid an annual tax of more than five Korean Won, meaning that only Japanese and Korean citizens of considerable wealth were able to vote. As a result, majority of the advisory council members were Japanese and pro-Japanese, Koreans.

Japan claimed that the laws and system under its colonial rule complied with its assimilation policy, but this was far from the truth. Japan believed it was dangerous to grant people in Korea the same political rights as their own citizens, which is why it was never seriously considered by the Government-General. The fraudulent local autonomy the Government-General introduced to stabilize the administrative system only cultivated pro-Japanese collaborators and created a national divide in Korea.

⟨Reference 1⟩ Diary of Yun Chi-ho, a Proactive Collaborator with the Japanese

"From nine in the morning to six in the afternoon, I attended the economic council meeting convened by the Governor-General. Only nine out of the forty-four invited to the meeting were Korean citizens. Their opinion, regardless of whether it was positive or negative, had no impact on the policies already established by the Government-General. They were practically deadwood."

May 13, 1933 (Saturday)

- Source: Kim Sang-tae trans. Yun Chi-ho ilgi, 1916-1943: *Han jisigin eui naemyeon sege reul tonghae bon sigminji sigisa* [Diaries of Yun Chi-ho, 1916-1943: A Glimpse into Colonial Korea Through the Personal Accounts of an Intellectual] (Seoul Yeoksa bipyeongsa, 2001), 311.

⟨Reference 2⟩ Jungchuwon, the Government-General Advisory Council (1920)

The *Jungchuwon* was headed by the inspector-general of state affairs and consisted of one vice-chairman, fifteen advisors, twenty *chanui* (government position), *a buchanui* (subordinate to a *chanui*), a secretary, an interpreter, and *a sokjeonim*. It also had a councilor and a *chamsa* present at each province to handle consultations with local officials.

- Source: National Institute of Korean History (History Net).

11

Increased Rice Production, Starving Farmers

Some argue that life in Korea improved during the Japanese colonial rule. The increase in average life expectancy and rice production are the two major factors that support this argument. Rice production increased under Japanese colonial rule, and is assumed to have allowed people in Korea to enjoy a better diet. Did the increased rice production actually lead to an improved dietary life for Koreans? Not at all. Most farmers in Korea starved as the majority of rice was taken away to Japan.

After Japan annexed Korea, Korea was delermined according to the market price of grains in Japan at the time. While food resources grew dependent on Japan, grains in Korea were utilized to maintain low grain prices back in Japan. For instance, when Japan dispatched a large number of troops to the Maritime Province of Siberia for a military expedition in 1918, it caused a drainage of rice in Japan which was large enough for the price of rice to surge, leading to the eruption of rice riots in Japan. To appease the unhappy rioters in Japan, Japan supplied rice from Korea and left Korea to suffer from an extreme shortage of food.

As domestic demand for rice rose in Japan, a plan to increase rice production in Korea was carried out in the 1920s. Irrigation facilities

〈Reference 1〉 Joseon's Rice Production, Export, and Consumption in the 1920s
(Production & Export: one thousand *seom* = 144,000kg, Consumption: one *seom* = 144kg)

Year	Production	Export to Japan	Consumption per Capita	
			Joseon	Japan
1920	12,708	1,750	0.63	1.12
1921	14,882	3,080	0.67	1.15
1922	14,324	3,316	0.63	1.10
1923	15,014	3,624	0.65	1.15
1924	15,174	4,722	0.60	1.12
1925	13,219	4,619	0.52	1.13
1926	14,773	5,429	0.53	1.13
1927	15,300	6,136	0.52	1.09
1928	17,298	7,405	0.54	1.13
1929	13,511	5,609	0.45	1.11
1930	13,511	5,426	0.45	1.08

- Source: Joseon migok yoram [Handbook of Korean Grains].

were improved to transform fields into rice paddies in Korea. As a result, Korea produced more rice and exported a greater amount to Japan. The amount of rice exported to Japan exceeded the amount of rice produced in Korea.

Many farmers in Korea were devastated during this period. After being repeatedly exploited and hassled by the increasing number of landowners and burdened by the cost of improving irrigation facilities, farmers were forced to sell their lands and leave the countryside. They boarded trains for the abandoned called *gimin yeolcha*(棄民列車) and headed to

〈**Reference 2**〉 Tower of Rice Sacks to Celebrate the Construction of Gunsan Port in Jeolla Province (1926)

- Source: National Institute of Korean History (History Net).

Manchuria. The extensive export of rice to Japan led to a drop in the per capita consumption of rice in Korea, which amounted to less than half of that in Japan over the same period. People in Korea supplemented their food shortage with mixed grains from Manchuria.

The poor food circumstances in colonial Korea have been revealed through a study conducted on the change in the amount of per capita nutrient supplies over the course of a century between 1910 and 2010. According to the study, the per capita nutrient supplies rose in Korea until 1918, but continued to fall since then. By the 1930s, the amount was finally brought up to its previous level in 1910 when Japan annexed Korea. However, there was a sharp decline in the 1940s when the Pacific

⟨Reference 3⟩ Change in the Daily Amount of Per Capita Nutrient Supplies in Korea (1910-2010)

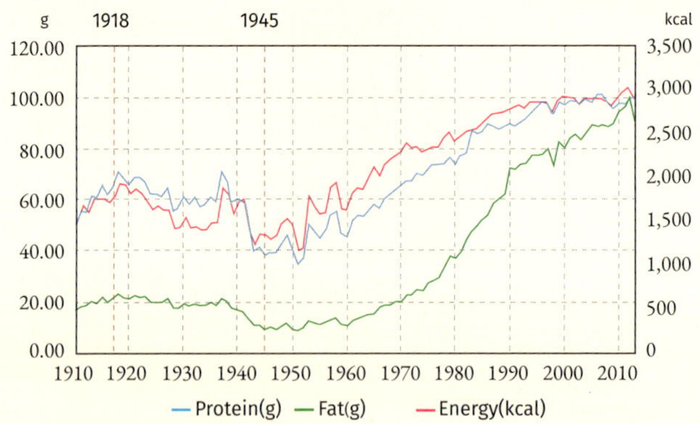

- Source: Yook So-young, "Sikpeum sugeuppyo bunseok e euihan 20 segi Hanguk saenghwal sujun byeonhwa e daehan yeongu" [A Study on the Changes in the Standard of Living in the 20-Century Korea through an Analysis of Food Balance Sheets], Doctoral Dissertation (Chungnam National University, 2017).

War broke out. The study's data therefore demonstrates that the people of Korea suffered from starvation under Japan's colonial rule.

The plan to increase rice production and the distribution of fertilizers may have led to a rise in Korean rice production under Japanese colonial rule, but an amount greater than the increase in production was taken away to Japan. Not only was the per capita consumption of rice in Korea half of that in Japan, people in Korea were poorly nourished. Cheap Korea rice was therefore a key requisite to sustaining Japan's capitalist system and enabling a colonial division of labor between Japan, Korea, and Manchuria.

12

Equal Workload, Different Wages

Japan claimed that under the slogan "*ilsi dongin*," everyone will be treated the same without discrimination in colonial Korea. Did the people of Korea and Japan actually receive equal treatment after Japan's forced annexation of Korea? The Government-General's official statistics show that wage discrimination clearly existed between the Korean and Japanese workers. In the case of carpenters, wages differed depending on what the carpenter made, and wage discrimination based on ethnicity clearly existed.

According to the Government-General's statistics, slight wage differences occurred depending on the location of work, but ethnicity caused a far greater gap in wage. Such gap was more prominent in cases where Korean and Japanese workers were in the same profession, proving that ethnicity carried much more weight in determining wages than the location of work and level of technical proficiency. For instance, there was

⟨Reference 1⟩ Wage Gap Between Ethnicities in 1925 (Government-General Statistics

			Gyeong seong	Mokpo	Dae gu	Bu san	Pyong yang	Sinuiju	Won san	Cheon gjin	Average
Carpenter	Furniture	Japanese	3.53	3.50	3.45	3.24	3.74	3.50	3.60	3.80	3.55
		Joseon	2.10	2.60	1.65	2.00	1.80	1.50	1.93	2.50	2.02
		Chinese	2.10	-	-	2.45	-	1.20	-	-	1.91
	Windows & Doors	Japanese	3.53	3.00	3.45	3.26	3.70	3.50	3.53	3.90	3.48
		Joseon	2.10	2.15	1.65	2.00	1.80	1.50	1.53	2.50	1.90
		Chinese	2.10	-	-	2.50	-	1.20	-	-	1.93
	Ships	Japanese	3.70	3.43	-	3.26	3.91	3.50	4.66	4.50	3.85
		Joseon	2.60	2.70	-	-	1.79	1.50	2.25	3.00	2.31
		Chinese	2.00	-	-	-	-	1.20	-	-	1.60

- Source: Statistical Yearbook of the Japanese Government-General of Korea (1925).

a distinct gap between the Korean and Japanese workers in plastering, a job that requires expertise, and that gap only widened over time. The clear gap in the wages for jobs which required no expertise demonstrated that ethnicity rather than the level of technical proficiency was the excuse for discrimination. Korean laborers were paid approximately forty percent of the wage Japanese laborers received.

Regardless of whether they worked in rural or urban settings, wage discrimination between the Korean and Japanese workers occurred commonly and naturally in colonial Korea. As Japan solidified its

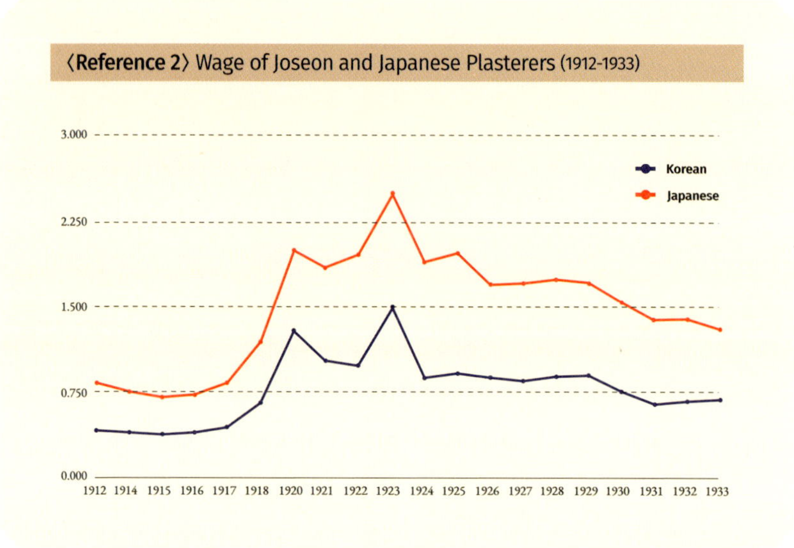

rule over Korea, the Korean workers were assigned to low-paying, unsophisticated jobs instead of occupations that required expertise. Meanwhile, a diverse wage structure became established for Japanese workers according to their experience and occupation. Hence, wage discrimination ultimately led to occupational discrimination in colonial Korea.

Most of the Koreans were subject to unsophisticated labor also meant that Korean workers faced extremely harsh working conditions. Workers who physically struggled to adapt to such conditions were often punished and suffered pay cuts. These discriminations based on ethnicity eventually gave rise to strikes. Such strikes increased and intensified over the course of the March First Independence Movement forcing Japan to mobilize its police forces.

〈Reference 3〉 Outbreak of Strikes (1912-1932)

Year	No. of Strikes	No. of Participants	Year	No. of Strikes	No. of Participants	Year	No. of Strikes	No. of Participants
1912	6	1,573	1919	84	9,011	1926	55	5,784
1913	4	487	1920	81	4,599	1927	81	10,523
1914	1	130	1921	36	3,599	1928	94	7,759
1915	9	1,951	1922	36	1,799	1929	119	8,293
1916	8	458	1923	46	6,041	1930	46	18,972
1917	8	1,148	1924	72	6,725	1931	72	180
1918	50	6,105	1925	45	5,700	1932	45	14,824

- Source: Japanese Government-General Police Bureau, *Joseon gyeongchal gaeyo* [Overview of the Joseon Police].

〈Reference 4〉 Labor Union Protest During the 1929 Strike in Wonsan

- Source: National Institute of Korean History (History Net).

13

Massacre in Joseon

Japan stated that no massacres were committed in Korea during its colonial rule. At the time, Japan was striving to prove the legitimacy of its rule over Korea by comparing it to the colonies of Western imperialist powers. However, Japan's justification distorted and fabricated the truth about its colonial rule of Korea. Japan in fact used force to incapacitate the people of Korea. Many independence activists as well as civilians were murdered in the process.

To dominate Korea, Japan brutally slaughtered people of Korea in the Donghak Peasant War and battles with the Korean righteous armies. During the March First Independence Movement in 1919, the military and police were mobilized to repress non-violent protests with guns and swords. Shots were indiscriminately fired at protesters and a massacre occurred at a village called Jeam-ri where the residents were burned to death inside a locked church building. According to

Hanguk dongnip undong jihyeolsa [A Bloody History of the Korean Independence Movement] by Bak Eun-sik, a total of 7,509 people were killed, 15,961 were injured, and 46,948 were arrested in the process of suppressing the movement. Even the Government-General admitted that hundreds of Japanese troops and policemen were sacrificed to suppress the independence movement. Such facts demonstrate the circumstances people in Korea suffered under the Government-General's rule. Japan's oppression did not cease there. Many Korean protesters were imprisoned and tortured to death (For further details, refer to the March First Movement database created by the National Institute of Korean History).

Japan's colonial rule depended on the authority of the Governor-General. As the de facto ruler of colonial Korea, the Governor-General was chosen among Japanese generals or admirals and was directly appointed by the emperor. Under the Japanese emperor's direct supervision, the Governor-General was able to wield absolute authority in colonial Korea. The Governor-General was not bound by the Japanese Constitution. Therefore he possessed the right to command the Japanese Army and Navy stationed in Korea, create ordinances that superseded the laws of homeland Japan, control overall administration in Korea, and oversee all branches of the Government-General including the judicial branch. This kind of authority allowed Japan to involve its troops, military police, and police in mercilessly suppressing activities of resistance and independence in Korea.

Apart from Korea, Japan also committed massacres in the Russian Maritime Province and the northeastern regions of China. Many Koreans were slaughtered by the Japanese military during the April Offensive and the Gando (Jiandao) Massacre of 1920. Japanese troops were dispatched to annihilate anti-Japanese armed forces in the Russian Maritime Province and the northeastern regions of China (Manchuria). Reports by troops who were dispatched at the time indicate that Koreans were defined as rebeis who were to be slaughtered in brutal ways. Koreans who were accused of leading or supporting independence movements were executed by the firing squad, while those who engaged in or escaped during armed resistance were shot to death. Koreans accused of participating in independence movements or raising funds for armed resistance were decapitated or stabbed to death. In addition, malcontent Koreans were to be decimated through torture, arson, rape, or by being buried alive.

On September 1, 1923, a great earthquake erupted in the Kantō region of Japan. Extensive damage from the earthquake exacerbated the public sentiment in Japan. To channel people's frustration elsewhere, the Japanese government turned the people of Korea into its scapegoat. They started a groundless rumor that people from Korea had poisoned wells in Japan, which caused thousands of Korea people in Japan to be murdered by Japanese soldiers, policemen, and vigilantes. Based on the investigations conducted by a correspondent, the news organ Dongnip sinmun of the Korean Provisional Government reported that a total of 6,661 people from Korea were killed during the massacre.

Japan reinforced its army and police to strengthen the grip over Korea and also began to separately manage independence activists. The 1925

Public Security Preservation Law established in Japan was implemented in Korea and the Ordinance on the Probation of Korean Political Offenders was promulgated in 1936 to constantly surveil independence activists. In 1941, independence activists were detained without trial based on the Ordinance on the Preventive Detention of Korean Political Offenders. Meanwhile, the Japanese government spent a considerable amount of funds on hiring spies who would collect information on independence activists to provide updates on independence movements. Such information was utilized in attempts to disintegrate the Korean Provisional Government or assassinate prominent Korean activists like Premier Kim Gu.

〈Reference 1〉 Burned Church in Jeam-ri

On April 15, 1919, the villagers of Jeam-ri were slaughtered after being herded into a church building that was locked and set on fire at a time when independence movements were taking place across Korea since March 1.

- Source: National Institute of Korean History (History Net).

〈Reference 2〉 Massacre of Koreans After the Kantō Earthquake (1923)

- Source: Sin Gi-su comp., Lee Eun-joo trans., *Hanil byeonghapsa* (1875-1945): *Sajin euro boneun guryok gwa jeohang eui geundaesa* [The History of Japan's Annexation of Korea (1875-1945): A Modern History of Humiliation and Resistance Through Photos] (Seoul: Nunbit, 2009), 277.

14

Distortions Through Colonial Historiography

How did Japan distort Korean history to justify and glorify its colonial rule? Japanese research of Korean history began in the mid-nineteenth century when Japan was developing aspirations of invading mainland China. Tokyo Imperial University played a central role in studying Korean history and by the late nineteenth century, such historical research served as a means for gathering the information necessary for realizing Japan's aspirations. Japanese scholars hence crafted the rationale that Korea historically deserved to be invaded and that Japan was in a position to provide guidance. Historical narratives based on this rationale are what Koreans commonly refer to as "colonial historiography."

Such colonial historiography was produced more actively after Japan's annexation of Korea in 1910. The purpose was to make people in Korea believe that Japan was superior to Korea in the aspects of military, economy, culture, and history. Japan knew people of Korea had a high pride in their history and heritage, which is why it sought to instill them with a sense of inferiority while instilling the Japanese with a sense of superiority. The organizations that took part in producing colonial historiography included the advisory council *Jungchuwon* and under the Government-General, the compilation committee *Joseonsa pyeonsuhoe*, and the Department of Law and Literature at the Keijō Imperial University. The Government-General's *Joseonsa pyeonsuhoe* thereby featured a colonial view of history through its publications such as the thirty-seven volume *Joseonsa* [History of Joseon] and *Saryo chonggan* [Compilation of Historical Sources].

Japan's colonial view of history justified its colonial rule and sought

〈Reference 1〉 Compilation Project of the *Joseonsa pyeonsuhoe*

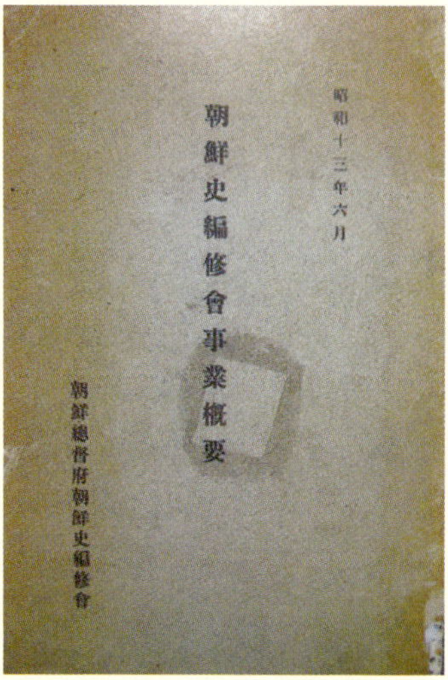
昭和十三年六月
朝鮮史編修會事業概要
朝鮮總督府朝鮮史編修會

Under the belief that a nation cannot perish unless its creed and history ceases to exist, Bak Eun-sik published Hanguk tongsa [Painful History of Korea] in Shanghai in 1915. Alarmed by the publication, Japan created a compilation division within Jungchuwon the same year to compile Joseon bandosa [History of the Joseon Peninsula]. A decade later in 1925, the Joseonsa pyeonsuhoe [Joseon History Compilation Committee] was launched and became responsible for compiling and distributing a distorted portrayal of Korean history titled Joseonsa [History of Joseon].

to discourage the people of Korea from taking pride in their own history and to indoctrinate them into accepting Japanese colonial rule. The following offers a summary of the main ideas behind Japan's colonial view on history.

• Inability to Achieve Autonomous Development (Heteronomy)

The originality, autonomy, and proactiveness of Korean history were negated in order to argue that developments in Korean history did not occur autonomously, but heteronomously by external forces. This argument based on geographic determinism considered Korean history as an extension of Manchurian history and highlighted the ancillary, peripheral nature of the Korean peninsula throughout history. The explanation that flunkeyism settled down in Korea from being constantly swayed by external powers was devised to quash Korea's desire for independence.

• Stagnant Nature (Identity)

Korea was defined as a historically stagnant society, which served as an excuse for colonial rule resembling the rationale that Western powers advanced as they invaded Asia. Fukuda Tokuzo supported the rationale by claiming that a feudal system similar to that of medieval Europe once existed in Japan but not in Korea. He Claimded that Korea compared to Japan, was underdebeloped by a millennium. Thus, Japan argued that a developed country like itself should be in control of underdeveloped countries like Korea.

• Common Ancestry

Japan allegedly ruled the Korean peninsula since the ancient times, which is why people in Japan and Korea were of common descent. Korean and Japanese people shared many similarities in language, culture, and physical appearances since their ancestors were same. Despite having the same ancestors, Koreans were not seen or treated as equals to Japanese people. This argument was later developed into theories that Empress Jingu conquered the three ancient Korean kingdoms or that the Yamato government of Japan once established a military outpost in Korea. These theories on precedents of Japanese rule over Korea were utilized to justify colonial rule over a country that shared ancestral, historical, and linguistic commonalities.

• National Traits

Political factionalism during the Joseon dynasty was pointed out as a chronic malady. This belief led to outcomes like the *Minjok gaejoron* by Yi Gwang-su, which justified colonial rule by blaming the national traits of Korea as the reason why it became a Japanese colony.

〈Reference 2〉 Books Featuring Japan's Colonial View of History: *Nissen dōsoron*(日鮮同祖論), Chōsen-shi (朝鮮史), *Naisen ittairon no kihon rinen*(內鮮一体論の基本理念)

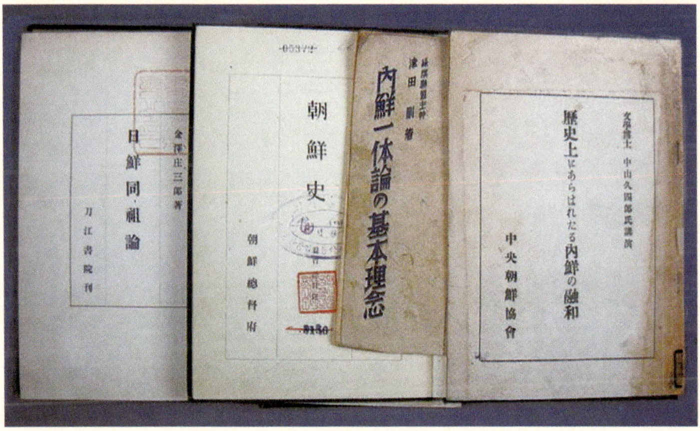

- Source: *The Independence Hall of Korea* Collection Brochure.

15

An Inferior Nation

Hate speech seems to be prevalent in Japan nowadays. A bad habit can be difficult to shed considering the way the denigration of Koreans has persisted in Japanese society from past to present. During the Japanese colonial period, the people of Korea were denigrated at a national level. In other words, Japan actively created and spread negative impressions about the traits of Korea people, most likely because belittling them and dismissing their abilities was necessary for its colonial rule.

Japan recruited scholars to investigate the old customs of Korea. An outcome of this investigation was *Chōsenjin no shisō to seikaku* [The Thoughts and Character of Korea People] published by the Government-General in 1927. A substantial portion of the book's second chapter, which was on the character of Koreans came from *Chōsenjin* [The People of Joseon], a book published earlier in 1921 that was authored by Takahashi Toru who later became a professor at

〈**Reference 1**〉 Cover and Table of Contents of *Chōsenjin no shisō to seikaku*

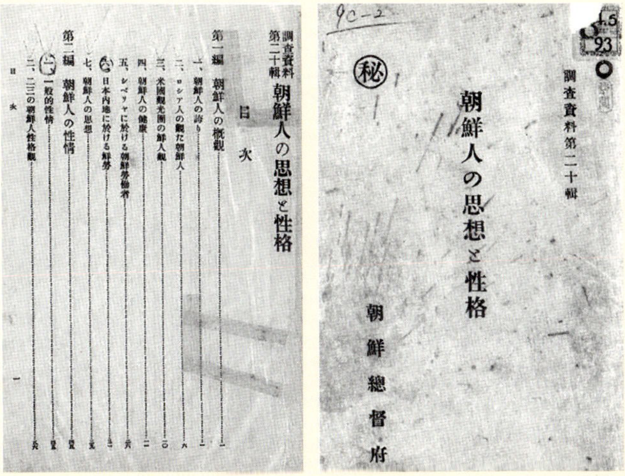

- Source: National Diet Library of Japan.

Keijō Imperial University. As quoted below, the book cited rigidity and dependence as the most fundamental traits of Koreans.

"Once they acknowledge a thought as their own, people in Korea stand by it until the end and willingly allow it to dictate them. An apt reflection of this rigidity in thought would be a Korean saying "Never try to change the old ways or establish new ways." To Koreans, there is no distinction between making improvements and changing for the worse so that reform is regarded as absolute evil.

This is how the book describes the dependent nature of people in Korea.

"All thoughts are dependent on China, which demonstrates that none of them feature an originality that is unique to Korea."

These descriptions show how Japan imparted the impression that people in Korea were incapable of realizing independence. Japan's state-level efforts to create and use negative impressions of Korea and use them to secure legitimacy for colonial rule caused Koreans to form a complex, self-deprecating portrait of themselves. On the other hand, negative impressions of Korean traits contributed to promoting positive impressions of the Japanese. For instance, unlike the earthquakes Japan often experienced, the Korean peninsula's geological features were static and thus regarded as a reason behind the rigidity of Koreans. The dependent nature of Koreans seemed unimaginable for the Japanese who formed a unique national polity led by their emperor. Such arbitrary comparisons helped Japan paint a dynamic and original portrait of itself.

After defining the character of the Korean people, the second chapter of *Chōsenjin* ends by highlighting the mercy Japan was showing Korea through its assimilation policy. Such mercy was a virtue absent in the West where racial discrimination was prevalent, a point mentioned to insist that Japan did not discriminate the people of Korea. However, developing derogatory arguments about the traits of people in Korea was none other than an act of discrimination on Japan's part. That is perhaps why hate speech persists to this day in Japan.

⟨Reference 2⟩ Cases of Discrimination in *Chōsen dōhō ni taisuru naichijin hanseishiroku* [Japanese Reflections of Joseon People]

Kim Gap-ji, who ran a junk shop in Gunsan, North Jeolla, was almost bitten by a dog when he stopped by a store to make a purchase. In a panic, Kim struck the dog's head with a bamboo stick. The Japanese store owner witnessed this and insulted Kim by declaring that "the dog was greeting you as its chum since you're a Korean. After all, Koreans are only as smart as dogs." This sparked a quarrel that took several people around them to break off.

Kim Cheon-byeong who sold tofu in Masan, South Gyeongsang shouted "Anyone need tofu?" in front of the house of a Japanese. A Japanese woman spitefully said, "Hey Yobo (a derogatory term referring to Korean people)! Can't you stay outside and ask? Did you have to open the kitchen door? I would never eat stinky tofu made by a yobo like you, not even for free. Who the hell would want to buy your stuff?"

* All names in the book are fictitious.

- Source: Lee Jeong-uk and Byeon Ju-seung eds., *Josenjing ege geureojima* (Seoul: Heureum, 2017), 112-151.

Chōsen dōhō ni taisuru naichijin hanseishiroku was published by the Japanese military police headquarters in April 1933. The book documents sixty-eight cases of discrimination the Japanese committed towards Korean people between April 1932 and March 1933. Japan's state-level efforts to denigrate the people of Korea caused the Japanese people living in Korea to discriminate against Koreans to a degree that concerned the Japanese military police headquarters in Korea.

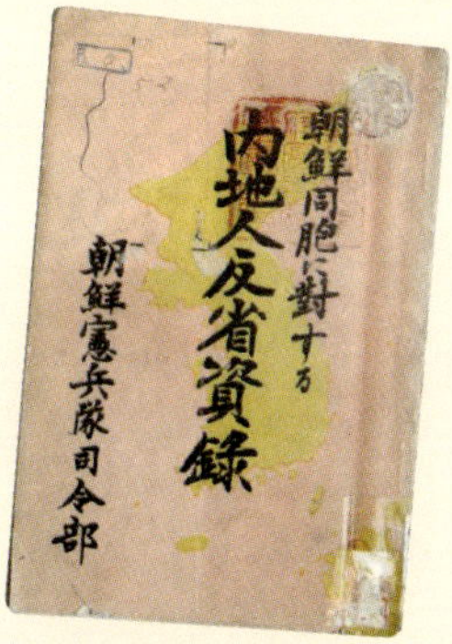

Chōsen dōhō ni taisuru naichijin hanseishiroku
- Source: National Library of Korea.

16

Vandalism of Cultural Heritage

Japan researched the customs and institutions of Korea to use the knowledge to its advantage in quashing colonial Korea's desire for independence. A law research bureau was established in 1908 to oversee research projects until such projects were transferred to the Government-General's interrogation bureau in 1910 and then later to the advisory council *Jungchuwon* in 1915. Although the initial scope of the research was limited to civil and commercial affairs, the scope gradually broadened to all aspects of everyday life in Korea including religion and feng shui. Such research produced various reports like *Joseon eui gwisin* [Ghosts in Joseon], *Joseon eui jeombok gwa yeeon* [Divination and Prophecy in Joseon], *Joseon eui pungsu* [Feng shui in Joseon], and *Joseon eui yusa jonggyo* [Pseudo-religions in Joseon].

Meanwhile, to maintain its colonial rule, Japan did not hesitate to distort or destroy the native cultures and heritages of Korea. Vandalizing palaces served the dual purpose of damaging the traditional culture of Korea and undermining the imperial family's authority. After forcibly occupying the Empire of Korea in 1910, Japan sold many of the buildings in Gyeongbokgung Palace so that a considerable number of them were either transformed into Japanese restaurants or temples or moved to Japanese residences in neighborhoods such as Namsan-dong, Pil-dong, and Yongsan in Seoul. In 1915, many palace buildings were demolished for the Korea Industrial Fair held to celebrate the fifth anniversary of Japanese colonial rule. The demolition cleared up enough space to build an exhibition hall of seventeen thousand square meters and decorate the garden outside the hall with stone pagodas and Buddha statues brought from all over the Korean peninsula.

The following year, the Government-General Building's construction began at Gyeongbokgung Palace. Hongnyemun Gate on the front side of the palace as well as the corridors on both sides of the gate were demolished and Geumcheonguo Bridge was razed. By 1926, the Government-General Building's construction was finished, leaving an overwhelming and obstructive structure to stand upon the palace's central axis running from north to south. The palace's original layout was completely destroyed in September of the following year when Gwanghwamun Gate at the palace entrance was moved to north of the Geonchunmun Gate on the east side of the palace. In 1932, Seonwonjeon, which was built to the northwest of Geonchunmun Gate to the portraits of all former kings, was torn apart. Parts of Seonwonjeon were used to build a temple (Bakmunsa) to the east of Jangchungdan Park in order to memorialize Itō Hirobumi.

Gyeongbokgung was not the only palace to be vandalized for symbolizing Japan's the absolute authority over the Joseon Dynasty and the Empire of Korea. In 1907, when Japan forced Emperor Gojong to abdicate for secretly sending envoys to the Hague, Hague, they had the crown prince Sunjong accede to the throne and move to Changdeokgung Palace in order to separate him from Gojong who resided in Gyeongungung Palace. Then, under the pretext of consoling Emperor Sunjong, Japan began to transform Changgyeonggung Palace into a park with a zoo and a botanical garden. Thousands of cherry blossoms, which happened to be a Japanese favorite, were planted around the palace grounds. At the spot where *Jagyeongjeon* once stood, a Japanese style building named *Jangseogak* was raised as a library equipped with a room to display all sorts of animal and plant specimens. Once *Changgyeonggung* Palace was turned into a park, the pro-Japanese Prime Minister Yi Wan-yong declared that it was Emperor Sunjong's wish to "open the palace to the public to provide consolation and serve as an educational facility." However, the Korean emperor's wishes had nothing to do with the decision that had already been made when the palace's transformation began. In 1911, shortly after Korea's annexation, the name of the palace was changed from *Changgyeonggung* to *Changgyeongwon* and thereafter served as a venue for many industrial fairs and exhibitions. Such events were publicized as "the largest in the Orient" and made Korea (Empire of Korea) appear more insignificant and obsolete by juxtaposing a "rising empire" with a "waning nation."

Hwangudan(Wongudan) was symbolic to the Empire of Korea as the place where King Gojong's enthronement as emperor was held. Japan demolished *Hwangudan* to build a railroad hotel (presently the Westin Chosun Seoul) for the South Manchuria Railway Company. Once Emperor Gojong passed away, Japan demolished and sold most of the buildings at the Gyeongungung (Deoksugung) Palace. The palace sustained further damage when it was turned into a park and opened to the public in October 1933. *Seokjojeon* turned into the Deoksugung Palace Museum to display modern Japanese art. When a west wing was added to *Seokjojeon* in 1938, the building became the Yi Royal Family Museum. In 1935, a zoo was created on the spot where the building *Dondeokjeon* used to stand, and in the fall of the same year, an exhibition featuring chrysanthemums, the symbol of the Japanese royal family, was held. Meanwhile, Gyeonghuigung Palace was demolished to build a school and Honghwamun Gate at the palace entrance was sold to *Bakmunsa* to serve as the temple's front gate.

Palaces were spaces where rulers of the Joseon Dynasty (Empire of Korea) resided and administered state affairs. Such cultural heritages representative of a dynasty which lasted for five centuries suffered mutilations as the Government-General headquarters became placed at the foreground of a palace while another was transformed into a park, all because Japan sought to visually demonstrate its authority as the new ruler and simultaneously undermine the stature of the Joseon royal family.

〈Reference 1〉 Government-General Headquarters at Gyeongbokgung Palace

A glimpse of the Government-General Headquarters being constructed at Gyeongbokgung Palace. Photographed by Okada Mitsugi(岡田貢). From the *Joseonsa pyeonsuhoe* Photographic Plate Collection.

- Source: National Institute of Korean History (History Net).

〈Reference 2〉 Front Views of Wongudan and Hwanggungu

Wongudan originally housed an altar where rites to heaven were performed. It was built in 1457, removed in 1464 after the final rite was held, and then rebuilt in 1897 to hold King Gojong's enthronement as emperor. Once Japan demolished it in 1914, the Westin Chosun Hotel came to occupy the site. All that is left of Wongudan is the octagonal three-story pavilion called *Hwanggungu* standing upon a granite stylobate.

- Source: Left - National Institute of Korean History (History Net),
Right – Seoul teukbyeolsisa pyeonchan wiwonhoe, *Ilje chimnyak araeseo ui Seoul* (1910-1945) [Seoul Under Japanese Aggression (1910-1945)] (Seoul: Seoul Metropolitan City, 2002), 309.

17

Plundered Cultural Assets

In the early twentieth century, imperialist powers appeared to be in a race to plunder cultural assets all over the world. Just as the museums in Britain and France exhibit more Greek and Egyptian cultural assets than the countries where such assets originated from, it is not surprising that so many of Korean cultural assets ended up in Japan. At present, there are 67,000 cultural assets related to Korea in Japan, among which 111 of them being either of great significance or designated as a national treasure. Because Korea defines cultural assets taken away to Japan under Japanese colonial rule as "plundered assets", Korea has been demanding for their return and is still waiting.

Japan began to exert state power to plunder Korea's cultural assets around the outbreak of the First Sino-Japanese War in 1894. Right before declaring war against China, the Japanese Army broke into Gyeongbokgung Palace on July 23, 1894, to plunder goods, treasures, and rare items passed down to Korean kings, and shipped them off to Japan from Incheon Port. Once the war began, a court adviser named Kuki Ryuichi, who also served as the director of the Imperial Museum, distributed the "Methods for Collecting Qing Treasures During War" to high-ranking officials of the Japanese government, army, and navy. These set of guidelines justified collecting the "essence of Oriental treasures" through the war to raise the prestige of Japan and enable it to become an academic hub in the East. Hence, war was considered an opportunity for Japan to obtain masterpieces that would normally be unobtainable. The guidelines stipulated that the plundering of cultural assets had to be overseen by the minister of the Japanese Army, Navy, or an army commander, and that the collected assets were to be kept at the Imperial Museum. This suggests that using military resources to plunder cultural assets was a state project for Japan.

Itō Hirobumi was the first to head the Japanese Residency-General that controlled Korea's internal affairs. Itō was also a known collector of porcelain, so during his time in Korea, he sought to acquire as many of them as possible. This motivated grave robbers to dig up tombs all over the country. The royal tombs in Gaesong became riddled with holes as robbers continued their merciless pursuit of burial goods, which angered the locals around the area. Itō then selected the finest 103 items out of all he acquired in Korea and presented them to Emperor Meiji in Japan.

After depriving Korea of its sovereignty in 1910, the Government-General used his power to overtly plunder Korea's cultural assets. It launched a survey of Korean historical remains and used the survey as an excuse to determine the state of Korean cultural assets and conduct excavations. The survey led to black-market dealings of robbed burial goods. Large-scale thefts were common at royal tombs in Gaesong and Gyeongju. The graves of peoples' ancestors were officially and unofficially destroyed just for the goods buried inside them. It is documented that "tombs were ravaged to the point where almost none of them remained intact."

Even low-ranking officials of the Government-General were involved in robbing Korean royal tombs. In 1926, a Government-General official named Moroga Hideo was arrested for being directly involved with a grave robbery and received a sentence of suspension. An invaluable artifact from the tomb *Geumgwanchong* was stolen from a storage unit in Gyeongju and ended up in the hands of Moroga who had been in charge of managing the storage. Some of the other artifacts Moroga collected around the time are now being kept at the Tokyo National Museum.

Sekino Tadashi was a Japanese scholar commissioned by the Government-General to survey buildings in Korea. Sekino assigned a grade to each building. He classified many historical buildings as inferior including Gyeonghuigung Palace, which was consequently taken apart by the Government-General and used to build Gyeongseong Middle School for the Japanese students. Heunghwamun Gate on the south side of the palace was used to serve as the front gate of the temple Bakmunsa built to commemorate Itō Hirobumi.

During the colonial rule, Japan used its power to conduct a survey of Korean historical remains and an individual's hobby and predilection.

This resulted in the plundering of Korean cultural assets under the protection of armed policemen. Developing an awareness of the background and circumstances related to the creation of historical materials and cultural assets is necessary in order to understand their true worth.

〈Reference 1〉 Front View of Bakmunsa Temple and Heunghwamun Gate

A front view of Bakmunsa Temple

- Source: Seoul Museum of History

The sign Gyeongchunmun (慶春門) is hanging from Heunghwamun Gate at the entrance of Bakmunsa Temple.

- Source: Jeong Seong-gil, Honorary Director of Keimyung University Dongsan Medical Center Museum.

〈Reference 2〉 Robbed Tombs

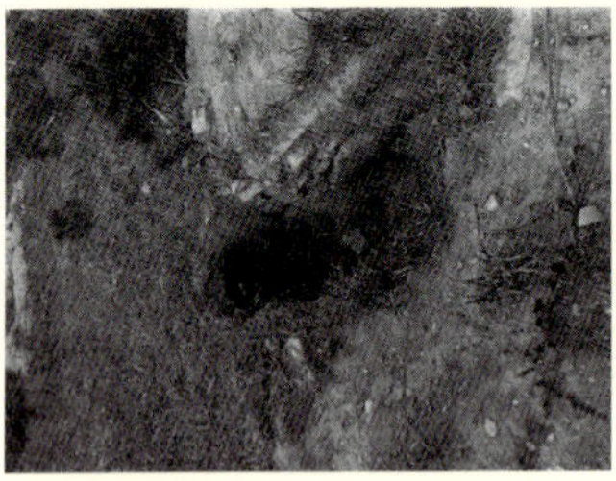

Robber's hole at Goryeo Gangneung in Ganghwa-gun, Icheon City

Robber's hole at an ancient tomb near the fortification in Songsan-ri, Bongsan-gun, Hwanghae Province

- Source: National Library of Korea.

18

Removed Japanese Flag, Halted Rotary Press

Ahead of the 2020 Summer Olympics, a photo of Son Gi-jeong with the caption "Marathon of the 1936 Berlin Olympics" was included in the "Japanese Gold Medalists" exhibition at the Japan Olympic Museum which opened in September 2019. A glimpse of the top of the Japanese flag in that photo seems to hint at the controversy over whether Son Gi-jeong should be remembered as a Japanese or Korean athlete.

The evening edition of Dong-a Ilbo on August 25, 1936 published a photo of the Berlin Olympic marathon winner Son Gi-jeong without the Japanese flag. The Government-General immediately banned the newspaper's publication and distribution. The 11 people allegedly involved in removing the flag from the photo including the journalist Yi Gil-yong and the artist Yi Sang-beom were brought in and questioned. The regional morning editions of *Joseon Jungang Ilbo* and *Dong-a Ilbo* on August 13 also published a photo of Son Gi-jeong without the

Japanese flag. The Government-General regarded the removal of the Japanese flag from Son's photo as an expression of Korea's national awareness and grew concerned that it might spark national solidarity among the people of Korea. As a result, eight *Dong-a Ilbo* staff members were arrested, and the publication was suspended for 279 days. *Joseon Jungang Ilbo* voluntarily suspended publication and eventually became discontinued.

Japan's control of the Korean press can be traced back to the 1904 Russo-Japanese War. During the war, Japan controlled the Korean press under the pretense of safeguarding military secrets. In November 1905, Japan deprived Korea of its diplomatic rights and installed the Japanese Residency-General gained control over domestic affairs in Korea. The Residency-General thereafter gained control over all publications including newspapers by establishing the Bylaw on the Confiscation of Newspapers in May 1908 as well as the Publishing Law in February 1909. Once Korea was deprived of its sovereignty in August 1910, most Korean newspapers were discontinued except for *Hwangseong Sinmun* and *Daehan Maeil Sinbo*. Even press activities by the Japanese were not allowed in colonial Korea, thereby drawing criticism from Japanese journalists like Tachibana Nao who worked as a Tokyo Asahi Shimbun correspondent in Gyengseong. This is what Tachibana openly stated about the Government-General's suppression of the press in Korea.

"Since the annexation, the Government-General established a policy to unify and eradicate Korean news agencies. The newspapers and magazines deemed appropriate were to be acquired, while those unaligned with Terauchi (Governor-General) were to be banned from publication. New publishing regulations to be promulgated required everything to obtain approval in advance. No new publications could be launched, and already existing newspapers and magazines were not allowed to relocate their office, change their name, or increase the frequency of their issues. Regarding the Government-General's policy towards the articles published by the new agencies, it can be described as either coercive, unyielding, absurd, or barbaric since it has mostly been outrageously uncivilized and oppressive." (Tokyo Asahi Shimbun, July 23, 1919)

By March 1919, the Korean peoples' discontent over Japanese oppression resulted in an outburst. Through a report drafted in July 1919 that examined the cause of the outburst and recommended precautions for governing Korea, the Japanese Army headquarters in Korea suggested that allowing freedom of speech could serve as a means to consolidate the ideas that the people of Korea were harboring and that exercising a moderate degree of control over the press could be useful to governing Korea. Based on the same rationale, Governor-General Saitō Makoto pushed for cultural politics. In 1920, the newspapers *Dong-a Ilbo* and Chosun Ilbo were launched. In 1922, the magazines *Gaebyeok, Sincheonji, Sinsaenghwal, Joseon jigwang* were launched. Japanese middle school textbooks at the time described that "the people of Korea have been allowed to a certain degree of freedom of speech, publication, and protest."

While the Government-General allowed newspapers and magazines to be published, it strictly censored the contents and confiscated or suspended them whenever anything detrimental to Japanese colonia rule was printed. During this time, *Dong-a Ilbo*, *Chosun Ilbo*, and *Sidae Ilbo* experienced about twenty confiscations a year on average. Confiscation was not limited to political articles. In May 1945, a piece written by a child expressing concern over the shortage of rice in Korea was confiscated.

The Government-General constantly controlled and sometimes placated the press of colonial Korea and this approach worked to a certain degree. However, as demonstrated through the removal of the Japanese flag from a published photo in August 1936, it was impossible to completely control the national awareness people of Korea shared. Once Japan began to launch full-fledged attacks on China in 1937, the Government -General began to enforce a policy of suppression towards the culture and language of Korea. In 1940, *Dong-a Ilbo* and *Chosun Ilbo* became discontinued.

〈**Reference 1**〉 International Olympic Committee Website

Son Gi-jeong is marked as a Japanese national, but the accompanying description reveals his Korean name and the fact that he was originally Korean.

Kitei SON / JPN

On 3 November 1935, Sohn Kee-chung of Korea (South Korea) set a world marathon record of 2:26:42.0. Because Korea was occupied by Japanese forces at the time Sohn's hopes for competing in the 1936 Olympics depended on his ability to qualify for the Japanese team. This he accomplished, as did fellow Korean Nam Seung-yong. Both young men were forced to adopt Japanese names (his participation is recorded under the Japanese name Son Kitei).

〈**Reference 2**〉

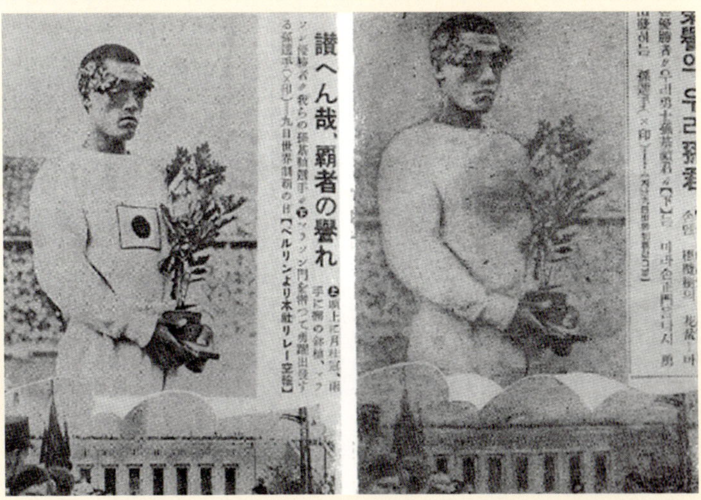

- Source: Son gi-jeong Museum. August 23, 1936 edition of *Osaka Asahi Shimbun* (Left), August 25, 1936 evening edition of *Dong-a Ilbo* (Right).

〈**Reference 3**〉 An article deleted by the Governor-General of Joseon upon inspection

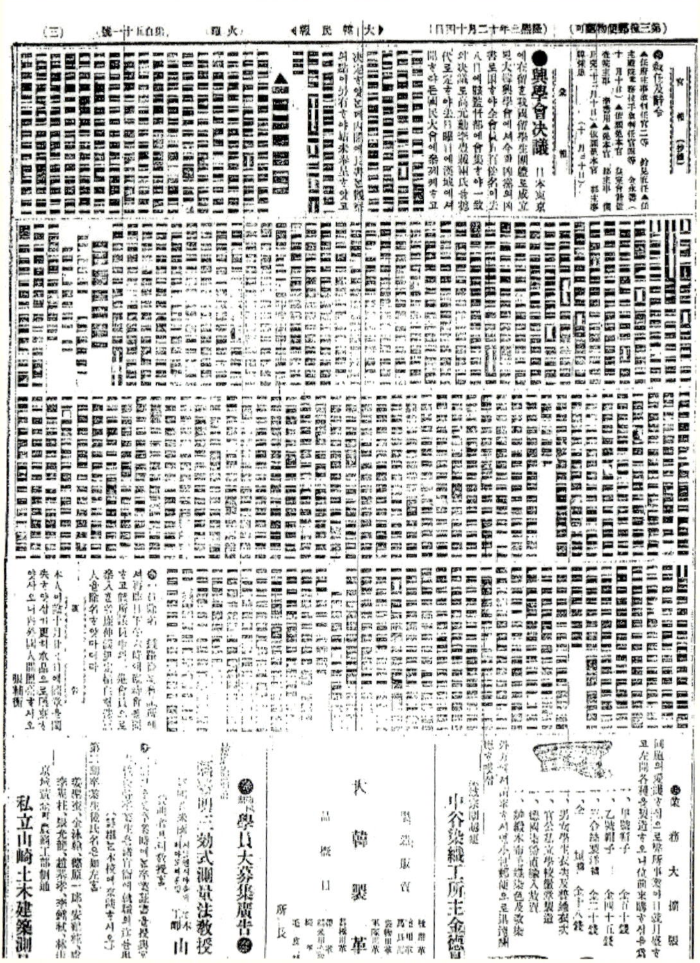

Daehanminbo(大韓民報) December 14, 1905.

- Source: The Independence Hall of Korea

〈Reference 4〉 Number of Newspaper Confiscations (1920-1940)

Year	Dong-a Ilbo	Chosun Ilbo	Jungoe Ilbo	Maeil Sinbo	Total	Note
1920	19	32			51	Dong-a Ilbo, Chosun Ilbo launched
1921	16	26			42	
1922	16	14			30	
1923	16	23			39	
1924	68	59	56		183	Sidae Ilbo launched
1925	67	66	44		177	
1926	35	58	32	3	128	Sidae Ilbo (27) changed name to Jungoe Ilbo (5)
1927	46	62	45	3	156	
1928	28	28	32	3	91	
1929	28	23	26	4	81	
1930	31	20	31	1	83	
1931	17	9	6	6	38	Jungoe Ilbo changed name to Jungang Ilbo
1932	7	8	5	4	24	
1933	6	10	7	1	24	Jungang Ilbo changed name to Joseon Jungang Ilbo
1934	9	4	4	1	18	
1935	2	3	3	5	13	
1936	9	13	8	6	36	
1937	2	8		8	18	
1938	5	7		5	17	
1939	8	5		3	16	
1940	1	3		2	6	
Total	436	481	299	55	1,271	Dong-a Ilbo, Chosun Ilbo discontinued

- Source: Jeong Jin-seok, *Geukbi Joseon chongdokbu eui eollon geomyeol gwa tanap* [The Government-General's Secret Censorship and Suppression of the Press in Joseon] (Seoul: Communication Books, 2008), 115.

19

Subjects of the Japanese Emperor: Oath of Imperial Subjects, Shrine Worship

The Japanization policies sought to transform the people of Korea into "loyal subjects of the Japanese emperor" so that they could be mobilized for Japan's wars of aggression. In 1931, Japan started the Liutiaohu Incident and began their invasion of northeastern China as the incident developed into the Mukden Incident. In 1937, Japan instigated the Lukouchiao Incident, which developed into the Second Sino-Japanese War. To engage in these acts of aggression, Japan intentionally used Korea as a logistics base. Therefore, it was necessary to secure the cooperation of the people in Korea through the Japanization policy that aimed at indoctrinating them with the idea that "Japan and Korea are one."

Minami Jirō, who began serving as Governor-General in June 1936, advocated three precepts for education in Korea: pledge absolute loyalty to the Japanese emperor, accept the idea that Japan and Korea are one, and nurture discipline and endurance. Through the third ordinance promulgated in 1938, curriculums in Korea were required to emphasize Japanese language and history, moral training, and physical education while the Korean language was banned in schools. The Oath of Imperial Subjects was drafted so that everyone in Korea was required to recite it by heart.

• Oath of Imperial Subjects (For Children)

1. We are subjects of the Great Empire of Japan.
2. We work together to devote our loyalty to His Majesty.
3. We endure and train ourselves to become excellent, strong subjects.

〈Reference 1〉 Students Reciting the Oath of Imperial Subjects

- Source: National Institute of Korean History (History Net); Seoul teukbyeolsisa pyeonchan wiwonhoe, *Ilje chimnyak araeseo ui Seoul* (1910-1945) (Seoul: Seoul Metropolitan City, 2002), 77.

The emphasis on loyalty to Japan and physical training was meant to prepare and mobilize Korean people for Japan's wars of aggression.

The policy of Japanization also forced people in Korea to worship at Shinto shrines. Chōsen Shrine erected at Mount Namsan in Seoul was a symbol of colonial rule and a central place in Korea for worshipping the Meiji Emperor. More shrines were built in other regions as well to facilitate worship. Schools that refused to worship at Shinto shrines suffered penalties or were shut down. Students were not the only ones forced to memorize the Oath of Imperial Subjects and worship at Shinto shrines. Ordinary people were also forced to worship at Shinto shrines and bow in the direction of Tokyo where the Japanese emperor resided. Some Christians organized a movement against worshipping at Shinto shrines, which resulted in the imprisonment and death of several participants including Pastor Ju Gi-cheol.

Japan declared that Japanization and promoting the idea that Japan and Korea are one were efforts to treat the people of Korea as equals as per the Japanese emperor's benevolent wishes. In reality, however, such efforts were aimed at obliterating the ethnic traits of people in Korea so that they could be mobilized in Japanese wars of aggression.

〈Reference 2〉 Chōsen Shrine at Mount Namsan

- Source: Seoul teukbyeolsisa pyeonchan wiwonhoe, *Ilje chimnyak araeseo ui Seoul* (1910-1945) (Seoul: Seoul Metropolitan City, 2002), 77.

〈Reference 3〉 Worshiping at Chōsen Shrine

- Source: National Institute of Korean History (History Net).

20

Subjects of the Japanese Emperor: Japanese Language and Names

When the battle with China after the Mukden Incident seemed to head toward a prolonged war, Japan indoctrinated the people of Korea with certain ideas to prepare them for mobilization. Governor-General Ugaki Kazushige advocated the idea that "Japan is in harmony with Korea" while his successor Minami Jirō insisted that people on the Korean peninsula must become loyal subjects of the Japanese Empire under the idea that "Japan and Korea are one."

Adopting Japanese names was a policy symbolic to Japanization. The Government-General's Bureau of Legal Affairs defined the policy's significance as "the fulfillment of the idea that Japan and Korea are one." The policy essentially sought to abolish the Korean system of clan-based surnames and introduce the Japanese system of household-based surnames. Under the Korean system of clan-based surnames determined by patriarchal lineage, women were allowed to keep their maiden surname after marriage. Clans, however, carried no weight in the Japanese system of household-based surnames so the married women and men who move in with their in-laws had to assume the surname of the head of their respective households. Under this family system of modern Japan, people were not allowed to join a household if their surname originated from a different household. The Japanese system thus sought to form a centralized structure placing the emperor at the top which would allow him to control each household through the head.

The policy of adopting Japanese names required the creation of household-based surnames, which was expected to disintegrate the clan-based system of Korea and produce subjects loyal to the Japanese emperor. Through the revision of a civil ordinance in November 1939, the Government-General announced that the head and the members of a family were to be addressed by the surname of their household and that the surname was to be determined by the head of each household. According to this revised ordinance, people in Korea were all required to create a new surname for themselves. Although Japan claimed that the adoption of Japanese surnames would grant the people of Korea an equal status as subjects of the Japanese emperor, the system continued to discriminate them based on their legal domicile listed in their family register.

The registration of Japanese names began on February 11, 1940, but only four percent of people in Korea filed for registration within the first two months. The resistance towards adopting a Japanese name was so strong that vowing to change one's surname came to be taken as the

〈Reference 1〉 An Article on the Adoption of Japanese Names

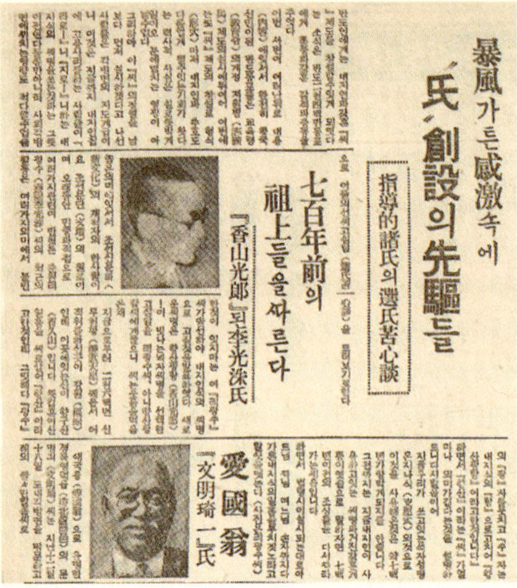

暴風가튼感激속에

氏創設의先驅들

指導的諸氏의選氏苦心談

七百年前의 祖上들을따른다

『香山光郎』된李光洙氏

愛國翁 『文明琦一』氏

The Government-General's bulletin featured an article introducing two figures who adopted Japanese names. Yi Gwang-su is described as a forerunner in adopting a Japanese name, which was Kayama Mitsuro (香山光郎). Mun Myeong-gi is described as a pro-Japanese who, apart from donating his plane to Japan, created his Japanese name Fumiaki Kiichiro (文明琦一郎) by adding two Chinese characters (一) to the end of his original name (文明琦).

- Source: Maeil Sinbo, January 5, 1940.

most serious statement of defiance. Japanese authorities had teachers and administrative agencies encourage the adoption of Japanese names. People who refused were denied admission to school or blacklisted as politically subversive figures. A Korean person in Dongnae, Busan who applied for the name Inunoko Suzuto (犬の子錫斗), which literally meant "the stone head of a bastard," was sentenced to six months in prison. Many clans collectively created surnames by transliterating their legal domicile into Japanese such as Kanaumi for Gimhae (金海) or Yanayama for Yangsan (梁山). By the time the deadline for registration arrived on August 10, 1940, eighty percent of people in Korea had applied. Japanization also entailed the everyday use of the Japanese language and a ban on using the Korean language. Studying the language and history of Korea was forbidden as well. The Korea Language Society's magazine *Hangeul* was discontinued in March 1942, and since October of the same year, members of the society were arrested and punished for violating the Public Security Preservation Law. Newspapers printed in Korean and published by Koreans like *Chosun Ilbo* and *Dong-a Ilbo* were discontinued in August 1940 because they "aroused national consciousness among the people of Korea and hindered them from becoming subjects of the Japanese emperor."

Hence, the Japanese policies of banning the Korean language and forcing the adoption of Japanese names were meant to erase the national identity of Koreans and to assimilate them into obedient subjects of the Japanese emperor.

〈Reference 2〉 Poster Compelling the Daily Use of the National (Japanese) Language

"To make troops great, use the national (Japanese) language everyday."

- Source: National Institute of Korean History (History Net).

〈Reference 3〉 Members of the Joseon Language Society (1946)

- Source: National Institute of Korean History (History Net).

21

Complete Mobilization of People and Supplies

World War I reshaped the previous understanding of war. Previously, the outcome of war hinged on which side had more well-trained soldiers. However, as tanks, fighter planes, and submarines appeared and trench warfare took place, wars became prolonged and required greater amounts of weapons, fuel, and combatants. This shift to total war made victory or defeat depend on which side had enough power and resources to fight longer. In the case of Japan, this change initiated a system of complete mobilization that took advantage of people and supplies in colonial Korea in order to engage in wars of aggression.

In July 1937, Japan's invasion triggered a war with China. As the war carried on, the Japanese government established the National Mobilization Law in April 1938 in order to efficiently mobilize all of its human and material resources. The law authorized the Japanese government to take control over labor resources, supplies, capital, industrial organizations, pricing, publishing, and the press, without having to obtain parliamentary approval. War was placed ahead of individual livelihoods. Individual thoughts and actions with the potential to hamper war efforts were regulated mercilessly. And such regulations were applied in Korea as well.

When the Pacific War erupted in December 1941, harsher regulations were enforced. Most young men were forced to go to war, causing labor shortages at factories and mines. As the war prolonged, Japan faced a shortage of troops and ran out of war supplies so that the gate (*torii*) made of copper and steel at Yasukuni Shrine had to be taken apart to produce war supplies. Japan thus turned the gaze to colonial Korean. All supplies, people, money, and even the soul of Korea seemed to be at Japan's disposal. Individuals had no choice. They were mobilized for war. They had to go wherever they were sent, be it a mine or battlefield.

The people of colonial Korea knew little about the law behind their mobilization. Considering that Japan's colonial rule itself was illegal, it did not matter which law served as a basis to mobilize them. Even if their mobilization had been legal under the system at the time, it did not change the fact that the people of Korea were coerced into mobilization through recruitment or government agencies. Between 1939 and 1945, approximately 7.8 million people in Korea were forcibly mobilized as laborers, soldiers, or civilian workers for the Japanese military. They were taken away to different parts of the Korean peninsula, Japan, southern Sakhalin, Southeast Asia, the Pacific Islands, Manchuria, and China to undertake the most toiling and dangerous tasks.

Japan collected a massive amount of resources from Korea to make

⟨Reference 1⟩ Extent of Damage from Japan's Forced Mobilization (Unit: person)

<table>
<tr><th colspan="3">mobilization of workers</th><th>Total</th><th colspan="2">mobilization of military personnel</th><th>Total</th></tr>
<tr><td rowspan="5">Within the Korean peninsula</td><td>Mobilization at the province level</td><td>5,782,581</td><td rowspan="5">6,488,467</td><td>Japan</td><td>7,213</td><td rowspan="5">59,668</td></tr>
<tr><td rowspan="2">Placement through government agencies</td><td rowspan="2">402,062</td><td>Joseon</td><td>12,468</td></tr>
<tr><td>Manchuria</td><td>3,852</td></tr>
<tr><td rowspan="2">National conscription</td><td rowspan="2">303,824</td><td>China</td><td>735</td></tr>
<tr><td>Southern front</td><td>35,400</td></tr>
<tr><td rowspan="5">Outside the Korean peninsula</td><td rowspan="2">National conscription</td><td rowspan="2">222,217</td><td rowspan="5">1,045,962</td><th colspan="2">mobilization of soldiers</th><th>Total</th></tr>
<tr><td>Army special volunteers</td><td>16,830</td><td rowspan="4">209,279</td></tr>
<tr><td rowspan="3">Quota-based recruitment/ Placement through government</td><td rowspan="3">823,745</td><td>Student volunteers</td><td>3,893</td></tr>
<tr><td>Army conscription</td><td>166,257</td></tr>
<tr><td>Navy(including volunteers)</td><td>22,299</td></tr>
</table>

- Source: Jung Hye-gyeong, *Ilbon eui Asia Tapyeongyang jeonjaeng gwa joseonin gangje dongwon* [The Asian-Pacific War and Japan's Forced Mobilization of Koreans] (Seoul: Northeast Asian History Foundation, 2009), 111.

up for food and supply shortages. Japan took forty-two percent of the rice produced in Korea in 1942 and sixty-three percent in 1944. In 1943, barley, wheat, and chestnuts were collected in addition to rice. Apart from food, Japan also collected a broad range of items from brassware and straw sacks to bells at churches or Buddhist temples. Even the bronze statue of the missionary Horace Underwood was taken away from the campus of Yonhi College. A rationing system was adopted to control necessities and food like rice. To secure minerals including alunite used to produce aluminum, 5,412 mines were developed across the Korean peninsula. The laborious burden of mining was of course left to the people of Korea to bear.

〈Reference 2〉 Grain Collection Poster

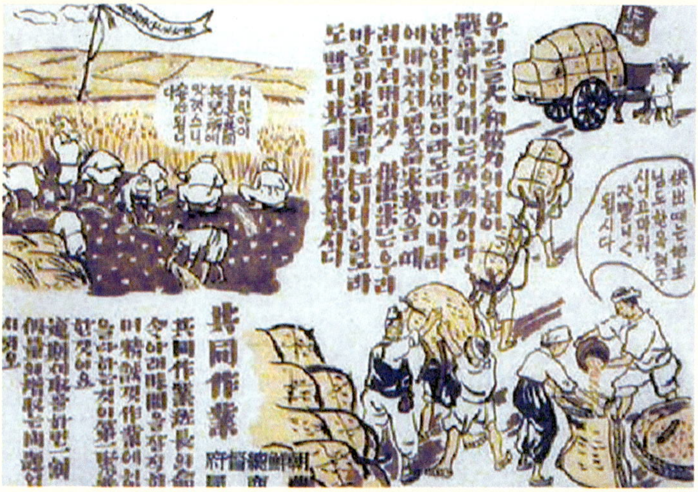

- Source: National Institute of Korean History (History Net).

〈Reference 3〉 Collected Brassware

- Source: National Institute of Korean History (History Net).

22

Workers Mobilized to Produce War Supplies

Some people argue that workers mobilized through corporate recruiters or government agencies cannot be considered to have been coerced into mobilization. Their argument is based on claims that such workers were not threatened into submission and were instead mobilized legally according to the National Conscription Ordinance. Did Korean workers freely choose to enter into employment? Certainly not.

The Second Sino-Japanese War that began in 1937 led to a shortage of manpower for Japan, which it attempted to replenish through forced mobilization in Korea. Such mobilization was justified by laws and regulations such as the National Mobilization Law (April 1938), the National Conscription Ordinance (July 1938), and the prescript "On the Relocation of Korean laborers to Japan." Article 2 of the National Conscription Ordinance stipulated that "unless there is a special reason, shortages in personnel can be replenished through employment agencies and other channels of recruitment." Hence, the ordinance did not serve as the legal basis for mobilization.

Japan adopted three different methods of mobilization: quota-based recruitment (May 1938-June1945), national conscription (October 1939-June 1945), and placement by government agencies (February 1942-June 1945). National conscription was initially utilized to fill technical positions, but its application broadened extensively since September 1944. What the three methods had in common was that the Japanese government adjusted and allocated the number of workers an employer (Japanese company) wished to hire people from Korea, which would then be finalized through consultations with the Government-General. All three methods therefore demonstrated organized mobilization based on government authority. Listed below are the procedures that the mobilization involved.

〈Reference 1〉 Steps for the Mobilization of Joseon Workers

	Step	Details
1	Labor Force Survey and Registration	The Government-General handles surveys and registration, then reflects the survey results in the labor mobilization plan each year.
2	Application	Japanese employers determine the number of workers they need and submit an application to the governor of their respective prefectures → The Japanese Ministry of Health and Welfare screens the applications and places a request to the Government-General in Joseon → Application documents are delivered to the Government-General

3	Mobilization	Government-General delegates mobilization tasks to each Korean province → Tasks are further delegated to administrative offices, police stations and substations, and influential figures of each county, town, township, and island as well as to relevant organizations (employment agencies, Korean League for the Total Mobilization of the National Spirit, Joseon Labor Association, Joseon Association of Civil Engineering and Construction) → Each town and township selects workers and processes the papers for their relocation → Selection results are collected and reported to the Government-General → Each town and township finishes preparations for transportation according to schedule
4	Transportation	The Government-General supervises transportation → Transportation is carried out by the Joseon Labor Association and reports back to the Government-General → The Government-General notifies relevant parties in Japan (employers, prefectural governors, Ministry of Health and Welfare) → Korean workers are delivered to their respective Japanese employer

- Source: Jung Hye-gyeong, *Jingyong gongchul gangje yeonhaeng gangje dongwon* [Conscription, Collection, Seizure, Forced Mobilization] (Seoul: Seonin, 2013), 17.

All the steps in the process of mobilization show that the administrative agencies under the Government-General's coercive system were heavily involved. Of course, some people may have headed to Japan voluntarily to escape the economic hardships they suffered in Korea. However, most Korean workers were mobilized through coordination between government forces. The workers were not sent to places where they wished to work at. Instead, they were forcibly mobilized to work wherever they were required by the government and companies in Japan.

The involvement of coercion depended on whether a person's free will has been respected or not. If the Korean workers' free will had been respected during recruitment and placement through government agencies, they would not have ran away before arriving at their places of employment. The number of workers who escaped was 2000 in 1939, which was 5.2 percent of all the workers mobilized that year. That percentage soon jumped to 37.2 percent by 1940 and 40 percent by 1943. To the workers who became mobilized, drawing a distinction between recruitment, placement through government agencies, and conscription was meaningless.

〈Reference 2〉 Mobilized Factory Workers

Mobilized workers assembled at Cheongju Station to be sent to work at the Nippon Steel Factory in Osaka.

- Source: Ilje gangjeomha gangje dongwon pihae jinsang gyumyeong wiwonhoe [The Truth Commission on Forced Mobilization Under the Japanese Imperialism], *Gangje dongwon gijeung jaryojip* [Collection of Donated Sources on Forced Mobilization] (2006), 68.

〈Reference 3〉 Site of Forced Mobilization (Hashima Island)

Hashima Island was one of the "Sites of Japan's Meiji Industrial Revolution" that collectively became inscribed on the World Heritage List on July 5, 2015. At the time, the Japanese Ambassador to UNESCO Sato Kuni pledged that "Japan is prepared to take measures that allow an understanding that there were a large number of Koreans and others who were brought against their will and forced to work under harsh conditions in the 1940s at some of the sites, and that, during World War II, the Government of Japan also implemented its policy of requisition." This pledge was expected to ensure an obvious display at the site about the fact that people from Korea and China as well as Allied prisoners were forced to work on Hashima Island. However, the pledge is yet to be fulfilled.

- Source: Northeast Asian History Foundation.

23

The Reality of Forced Labor

As explained in the previous chapter, careful planning and organized execution by public authorities were involved in forcibly mobilizing people from Korea. What kind of work were Korean workers assigned

〈Reference 1〉 Forcibly Mobilized Joseon Workers Being Physically Examined

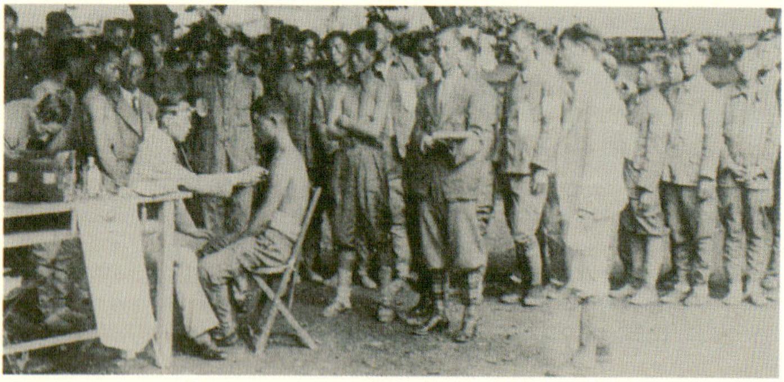

- Source: Hayashi Eidai, *Kesareta chōsenjin kyōsei renkō no kiroku* [Expunged Records of People Forcibly Mobilized from Joseon] (Tokyo: Akashi Shoten, 1989).

to and how were they treated? To answer this question, it is necessary to examine the places where mobilized people were sent to work. Below is a list of areas and workplaces Korean workers were sent.

〈Reference 2〉 Areas and Workplaces that Employed Joseon Workers

Region	No. of Workplaces	Major Workplaces
Korean peninsula	7,467	Coal mines, Mines, Ports, Munitions factories, Military construction sites, Civil engineering projects
Japan	4,119	Coal mines, Mines, Ports, Munitions factories, Military construction sites, Civil engineering projects
Southern Sakhalin	77	Coal mines, Lumbering sites, Civil engineering projects, Factories
Pacific	112	Coal mines, Military construction sites, Ports, Civil engineering projects, Factories, Farms
Southeast Asia	4	Factories (Steel Mills), Farms
Chinese Manchuria	316	Coal mines, Military construction sites, Civil engineering projects, Farms
Total	12,095	

- Source: Jung Hye-gyeong, *Ilje gangje dongwon pihae, ingan bopyeon eui gachi reul jikineun pyotdae* [Damage From Japan's Forced Mobilization and a Milestone in Defending Universal Human values] in *Hanil yeoksa jaengjeom: Ilje singmin jibae wa geukbok* [Historical Issues between Korea and Japan: Overcoming Japanese Colonial Rule] (Seoul: Northeast Asian History Foundation, 2019), 114.

Workers mobilized from Korea were placed at dangerous sites that posed life-threatening risks such as mines, ports, munitions factories, civil engineering projects, and military construction sites. With the concern that such risks could cause Korean workers to run away, the personnel responsible for mobilization refrained from offering information about the kinds of work the workers were expected to perform.

Moreover, Korean workers were already burdened with debt from the moment they arrived at their destination. They were forced to bear all the expenses for the transportation to their workplace as well as the tools, necessities, and room and board costs. Their debt was deducted from their monthly wage. Just as they were unaware of where they were being sent to, Korea workers were unaware that their debt was piling up. They were always notified after the injustices happened. This reveals the nature of Japan's mobilization that denied Korean workers the freedom to make their own choices.

⟨Reference 3⟩ A Mobilized Worker's Promissory Note

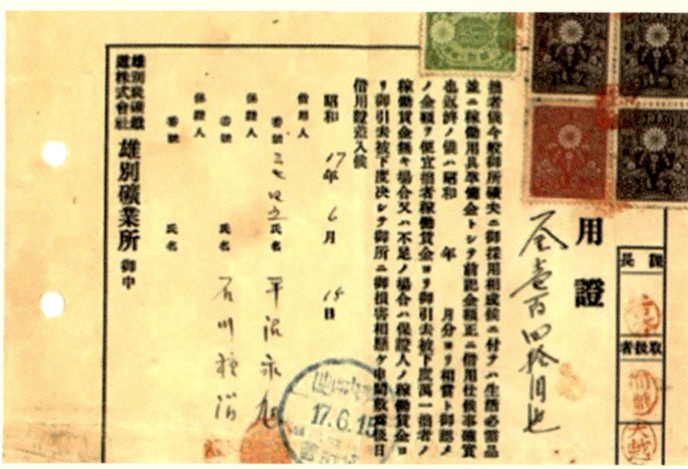

This promissory note was issued by Yun Yeong-uk who was mobilized to work at the Yubetsu Coalmine in Hokkaido, Japan. According to the note, Yun borrowed 140 Japanese Yen from the coalmine to purchase equipment and necessities and agreed to deduct the money from his future wages. Yun later testified that the company handed the note to him along with a blanket, hat, and clothes when he first arrived at the coal mine, and that he struggled to pay back the large debt with his wages.

– Source: The Truth Commission on Forced Mobilization Under the Japanese Imperialism.

Korean workers suffered unfair treatment in all aspects of their life on site. The testimonies that victims of forced mobilization gave offer glimpses of the harsh reality they faced, which was filled with life-threatening accidents, starvation, and unwarranted contempt. Serious violations of human rights occurred on a daily basis.

〈Reference 4〉 Testimonies of Forcibly Mobilized Korean Workers

(According to the investigation on the Numakura Hydroelectric Power Plant in Fukushima Prefecture) "the plant's construction began in July 1944 and was rushed to be completed by December. 712 Chinese workers were mobilized alongside thousands of Korean workers. Around ten Chinese fatalities occurred and details about Korean victims remain unknown. ... My compatriots slaved away from six in the morning until six in the evening. Meals were meager and most people had to work barefoot even when it snowed. Many starved or froze to death.

Bak Gyeong-sik, trans. Bak Gyeong-ok, *Joseonin gangje yeonhaeng eui girok* [Records of People Forcibly Taken From Joseon] (Seoul: Gojeuwin, 2008), 138.

"On February 3, 1942, a pit collapsed at the underwater Chosei Coal Mine in Yamaguchi Prefecture. Among the 183 workers who drowned, 130 were from Korea. Too many wooden supports had been removed. ... The company determined that it would be difficult to restore the coal pit, so it sealed the pit's entrance and ordered for a new pit to be dug. The 183 trapped inside the coal pit never made it back out. The Korean workers who were fortunate enough to avoid the calamity because they were off duty had to endure hell as they continued to mine coal at a different pit in the same waters where their colleagues had drowned."

Jung Hye-gyeong, *Ilbon eui Asia Taepyeongyang jeonjaeng gwa Joseonin gangje dongwon* [The Asia-Pacific War and the People Japan Forcibly Took from Joseon] (Seoul: Northeast Asian History Foundation, 2019), 123.

24

To the Battlefield: From Voluntary Enlistment to Conscription

"The maximum number of Army and Navy troops (ranked sergeant or below) in their third year of service who are of Yamato descent is estimated to be 1.2 million. This is a dismal estimation considering the number of troops that need to be deployed across Greater East Asia. In general, three years of service is already a heavy burden. If we utilize foreigners, we can secure 200,000 more troops by 1946 and further bring the number up to 400,000 in due course. Hence, considering the difficulty in maintaining a sufficient number of troops and the sacrifices our nation made, utilizing foreigners for our military strength is an urgent matter that needs to be put into action."

- Japanese Ministry of the Army, *A Review of Our Nation's Manpower in Light of the Great East Asian War* (January 20, 1942).

Since going to war with China in 1937, Japan realized that relying on

Japanese people alone was likely to impose limitations on sustaining the war effort. As the war spread to the Pacific, Japan needed more troops. However, it was impossible to mobilize further domestically. A new pool of human resources had to be uncovered to continue engaging in wars of aggression. This military demand caused Japan to "utilize foreigners," or mobilize its colonial subjects in Korea for war purposes.

In April 1938, Japan launched an Army Special Volunteer Program. Later, a student volunteer program was announced in October 1943 to recruit more soldiers. In April 1944, Japan enforced a conscription system. Japan was initially hesitant about handing guns to people in Korea through conscription due to the suspicion that the muzzle of those guns might point back to the Japanese. This suspicion made it necessary to minimize the resistance of the people in Korea ahead of carrying out conscription. Hence, the purpose of earlier volunteer programs was to secure legitimacy for conscription. In July 1943, the Ordinance on Navy Special Volunteers was promulgated, thereby expanding the volunteer program to the navy.

By using the word "volunteer," Japan made it appear as if these young men of Korea had been eager to serve in the army or serve as student volunteers. Japan was keen on encouraging people to volunteer and employed various methods of persuasion and coercion which included producing a film to promote the volunteer program. As a result, the number of applicants was about seven times greater than the number of volunteers recruited in 1938. This proportion continued to soar over the years to twenty-one-fold of the volume of recruitment in 1939,

〈**Reference 1**〉 A scene from *Volunteer*, a propaganda film released in 1941

Volunteer was a propaganda film about young Joseon man who became a volunteer and features the military song "A Volunteer's Mother" sung by Jang Se-jeong (Directed by An Seok-yeong, produced by Choi Seung-il).

forty-eight-fold in 1941, fifty-six-fold in 1942, and fifty-fold in 1943. Over the period of six years from 1938, a total of 17,644 were recruited through the Army Special Volunteer Program. Through the Navy Special Volunteer Program, 3,000 were recruited between 1943 and 1944. And the Student Volunteer Program recruited another 4,385 in 1944.

This was possible because recruitment quotas were allotted to each region and law enforcement authorities were mobilized. Through a survey in 1941, it was revealed that the majority of applicants were "pressured by government authorities into applying." Despite the fact that the survey was conducted by the Japanese government, only thirty-five percent of the survey's respondents indicated that their application had been voluntary. Through the conscription that began in 1944, 185,556 were mobilized in Korea.

〈Reference 2〉 Motive of Joseon People for Applying as Volunteers (1941)

	17yrs old	18yrs old	19yrs old	20yrs old	21yrs old	22yrs old	23yrs old	24yrs old	Above 24yrs old	Total
Voluntary	5,673	6,943	7,771	7,591	6,486	5,357	3,965	2,694	3,704	50,184
Pressure from government authorities	9,355	11,089	12,117	11,844	10,704	8,722	6,682	4,347	4,812	79,672
Other	1,925	2,012	2,318	2,125	1,747	1,610	1,132	1,146	1,190	15,205
Total	16,953	20,044	22,206	21,560	18,937	15,689	11,779	8,187	9,706	145,061

- Source: Byun Eun-jin, *Ilje singmin tongchi eui seonggyeok gwa Joseonin gunsa dongwon* [The Characteristics of Japanese Colonial Rule and the Military Mobilization of Joseon People] in *Ilbon gwa seogu eui singmin tongchi biyo* [A Comparison of Japanese and Western Colonial Rule] (Seoul: Seonin, 2004), 464.

〈Reference 3〉 Joseon Volunteers of the Japanese Army at Chōsen Shrine (July 13, 1942)

Joseon people mobilized as volunteers of the Japanese Army are worshipping at Chōsen Shrine.

- Source: *Ilje gangjeomha gangje dongwon pihae jinsang gyumyeong wiwonhoe* [The Truth Commission on Forced Mobilization Under the Japanese Imperialism], *Gangje dongwon gijeung jaryojip* [Collection of Donated Sources on Forced Mobilization] (2006), 68.

25

Yasukuni Shrine, a Spiritual Pillar for Wars of Aggression

Yasukuni Shrine is known for glorifying Japan's wars of aggression, but how is it linked to forced mobilization? 15years after Commodore Matthew Perry opened the ports of Japan in 1854, Yasukuni Shrine was built in 1869 following the Meiji Restoration to commemorate soldiers and civilian personnel of the military sacrificed during wars of aggression or civil wars such as the Seinan War. The shrine enjoyed an exclusive status because it was visited by the Japanese emperor.

After the Meiji Restoration, the emperor was considered to be a living god in Japan. Yasukuni Shrine imparted the idea that all wars launched at the emperor's command were holy wars, which meant that dying in such wars would be an honorable way to repay the emperor's kindness. The death of a father or brother on the battlefield was therefore not a cause for sorrow but joy because the deceased would be enshrined at a place where the emperor came to worship. Many youths were mobilized for the

〈Reference 1〉 Postcard of the Yasukuni Shrine

〈Reference 2〉 An Alchemy of Emotions Through Yasukuni Shrine

"As we remained prostrate, we had the honor of witnessing his majesty worship at the shrine. While not even racoons in mountains would shed a tear when humble, country folk like us die from a disease at the age of seventy or eighty, the sight of his majesty worshiping the war dead overwhelmed us with near-electrifying joy and gratitude. Afterwards, misery left our hearts and we felt much better at the thought that our children would live forever."

- Source: *Shufu no tomo* [Friend of the Housewife] (January 1944).

war in the hopes of becoming entombed at Yasukuni Shrine.

Once the Second Sino-Japanese War erupted in 1937, the war quickly spread across entire China. The Japanese military required more troops, which made it inevitable for people in Korea to be mobilized as soldiers. Hence, it became necessary to indoctrinate the people of Korea with the

〈Reference 3〉 An Editorial Urging People in Joseon to Support the War

"Spirits from the peninsula have been entombed whenever a special grand ceremony was held at Yasukuni Shrine, and this time, four have been entombed. There can be no greater joy or honor for a person from the peninsula. Since conscription has been implemented in Korea, men on the peninsula seem to be emulating the loyalty of their heroic predecessors who died protecting their homeland (Japan) and are trying to bravely overcome our national crisis. All that the twenty-six million people need to do is to emulate the determination of men on the peninsula heading to the battlefield, not to mention the noble spirit of sacrificing themselves to defend their homeland, and thus commit themselves to encouraging the will to fight or to boosting military strength. That is the best way to respond to the loyalty of the souls newly entombed at Yasukuni Shrine."

- Source: *Maeil sinbo*, October 24, 1944.

idea that it would be an honor for them to sacrifice their lives on the battlefield as soldiers fighting for Japan. Japan claimed that the people of Korea could also be entombed at Yasukuni Shrine if they died in battle, which was an honor worth voluntarily going to war. The prospect of immortality at Yasukuni Shrine drove nearly 21,000 people in Korea to death.

Yasukuni Shrine still maintains its belief that the forced annexation of Korea was to guarantee the security of Japan. It also claims that Japan invaded Korea through a legitimate process that did not involve force. Korea and Taiwan are missing from the list of the "countries that gained independence after World War II" displayed at the Yushukan Museum inside Yasukuni Shrine, which is an outright denial of historical facts that followed Japan's defeat.

The majority of people from Korea who have been arbitrarily deified at Yasukuni Shrine are victims who were forced into Japan's wars of aggression. They are still being used as a means to justify and glorify such wars despite Korea's independence. They are worshiped for sacrificing their lives on the battlefield for Japan, alongside war criminals responsible for starting the wars that took fathers and brothers away from Koreans. Korean victims are still being insulted and defamed because the shrine has been refusing to release them. The bereaved in Korea filed three lawsuits since 2001, demanding the release of their loved ones from Yasukuni Shrine. The fight continues to restore the honor of Koreans who died from being mobilized for Japan's wars of aggression.

〈Reference 4〉 Movement Against Yasukuni Shrine (2017)

Since 2006, Korean and Japanese citizens have been holding the event "Blaze of Peace! Light a Candle Against the Darkness of Yasukuni" every year in August.

- Source: Northeast Asian History Foundation.

26

Japanese Military Comfort Women Dragged to War

Some argue that women volunteered instead of being forced to serve as Japanese military comfort women. The argument is commonly made by the Japanese right wing in denial of the illegality of Japan's colonial rule. Is the argument valid? The answer is no. Comfort women victims were taken away against their will through the use of violence, deceit, and abduction. In 1978, when a Japanese person testified to being sent to North Korea after being tricked into traveling abroad, the Japanese government defined the case as an abduction committed by North Korea. Be it the use of violence or cajolery, mobilizing anyone against their will can be defined as having been forced.

During the Asia-Pacific War, the Japanese government and military planned, operated, and controlled the comfort women system under the pretense of efficiently engaging in wars. Government and military involvement in the mobilization of comfort women was acknowledged through the statement that the Japanese Chief Cabinet Secretary Kono Yohei made in 1993. In December 1937, the Japanese consulate general in Shanghai decided to create military comfort stations in consultation with the local military police and the Army attaché's office. Identity documents were issued to station operators so that they could recruit comfort women from Japan and Korea. In March 1938, the Japanese Ministry of the Army's aide-de-camp carefully selected station operators under the expeditionary army's control and arranged for the cooperation of military and local police forces in each region. From earlier that year, there were rumors of women having been conscripted or coerced into serving the Japanese military. Japan regarded such rumors as mere fabrications and punished for attempting to disrupt public order.

When the Asia-Pacific War began, the Japanese Ministry of the Army decided to install 400 comfort stations in areas where the war was happening in China, Southeast Asia, and the Pacific Islands. For instance, a station operator named Kitamura received a commission from the Japanese Korean Army headquarters and mobilized 22 females in Korea as comfort women. On July 10, 1942, those females joined the fourth dispatch of approximately 700 other comfort women who were sent from Busan Port to battlefields throughout Southeast Asia. The Japanese military bore all the expenses necessary for them to be delivered to the comfort station in Burma (presently Myanmar). Records indicate that even as Japan's defeat grew imminent, the Japanese military assigned quotas to the Government-General in 1945 for the mobilization of comfort women.

The spread of the war led to the mobilization of more soldiers. Accordingly, comfort women came to be recruited at a bigger scale in a more organized manner. As the war spread to Southeast Asia, violence and cajolery were equally used to mobilize women from Indonesia and Malaysia in addition to Korea and Taiwan. Even Dutch women staying in Indonesia were coerced into sexual slavery (Semarang Incident).

The Japanese government and military planned and carried out all matters pertaining to the mobilization of comfort women including the volume and the method of mobilization as well as the cost of recruitment and transportation. Under the comfort women system, women were taken away through the use of violence, intimidation, cajolery, and deceit. Kim Bok-dong was taken away to Guangzhou, China and then to Indonesia after the head of her village came and told her in 1941 that she was to work at a munitions factory as a member of the volunteer corps "Teishintai." Park Young-shim was taken away in 1938 as part of the "virgin quota" to be sent to Nanjing, Burma, and Yunnan. The only life, Bae Bong-gi knew was one of poverty until she was tricked into being sent to Okinawa in 1943 by a broker who told her that there was a place where she didn't have to struggle to make money.

Each step in the process of sending women to different comfort stations required cooperation from government authorities. Local police stations were involved in issuing identity documents for women sent from Korea or Japan to China after verifying the identity and purpose of travel. The Japanese government used ships for war to transport women. Employing cajolery, deceit, and intimidation to seize or kidnap someone and sending them to a region outside Japan violated Article 226 of the Japanese penal code. Trafficking minors under the age of twenty-one was a violation of international treaties. Yet, Japan paid no heed to such codes and regulations.

Despite attempts by the Japanese government and military to cover up the involvement of military or local police forces in transporting comfort women, many victims have testified that they were controlled by military or local policemen and suffered sexual violence or assault in the process of being taken to the comfort stations. Once they arrived at the comfort stations, women were subdued into sexual slavery. Comfort women were forced to follow military orders that determined where they could live, travel, and be tested and treated for sexually transmitted diseases. The women had nowhere to turn to as they suffered violence from comfort station operators, managers, and soldiers for being disobedient. They were neglected whenever they fell ill and had to rely on sheer luck to survive. They were deprived of their human rights to envision and chart their own destiny. Under the pretense of efficiently engaging in war, the Japanese government and military treated comfort women as military supplies instead of as human beings.

A total of 240 survivors have registered themselves as comfort women victims with the Korean government, which is but a fraction of the actual number of victims. The survivors have been telling stories that have not yet been documented in history, demanding historical justice and rehabilitation. Only twenty Korean survivors are left as of September 2019. The Japanese government is running out of time to sincerely apologize to the comfort women victims and take responsibility for their transgressions. The remaining survivors who stand for all the victims who already passed away or failed to reveal what they suffered could could be the last opportunity for the Japanese government to reinvent and devote itself to achieving peace in East Asia.

〈Reference 1〉 Drawing by Kim Sun-deok

Kidnapped and *Shipped Away*. Kim Sun-deok was a maid working for a wealthy family in Jinju until she heard rumor around 1938 that a Japanese factory was recruiting workers. She was seventeen when she was taken to Nagasaki, Japan and then transported to a comfort station in Shanghai.

- Source: Comfort Women Museum at the House of Sharing.

27

Defining Comfort Women as Sex Slaves

Were the Japanese military's "comfort women" sex slaves or not? This the question ultimately determines the nature of the history where women whose rights were violated under the comfort women system.

Terminology has been a hindrance to gaining a precise understanding of the Japanese military comfort women issue. The terms *jakbu* [hostess], *changgi* [prostitute], *nangjagun* [group of women], *teuksu buin* [special lady], or *chosenppi* [Joseon cunt] have all been used to refer to "comfort women" by the Japanese government or in military documents and memoirs by men who served in the Japanese military. Such terms were used because comfort women served as a means for the Japanese military to secretly provide "sexual comfort" to soldiers. To overcome this terminological obstacle, women in Asia convened in 1993 and adopted Japanese military "comfort women" as the official term (The Second Asian Solidarity Conference on the Issue of Military Sexual Slavery).

The term exposed the Japanese military's responsibility toward sexual mobilization to efficiently engage in wars and used quotation marks to clearly indicate that comfort women is not a term mindful of victims.

Meanwhile, the Korean Council for the Women Drafted for Military Sexual Slavery by Japan began using the term "sexual slavery" since the early 1990s as it drafted proposals and recommendations for the comfort women issue to be investigated by the United Nations Commission on Human Rights. There have been international efforts to resolve the issue of slavery since the 1920s and in 1926, 1926, and the definition of slavery was established through the Convention to Suppress the Slave Trade and Slavery. According to the first clause of Article 1 in the convention, slavery is "the status or condition of a person over whom any or all of the powers attaching to the right of ownership are exercised." The status or condition of subjugation is crucial to identifying slavery. A person in the status or condition of having been deprived of their freedom or autonomy by an entity with authority is a slave according to international law. The intent or means employed to drive someone into such a status or condition are not fundamental to the issue of slavery.

Since the 1990s, the concept of slavery grew more detailed through the process of attempting to resolve human rights violations that occurred during wars and armed disputes. Victims who suffered violations of their freedom or autonomy through sexual control came to be defined as sexual slaves. In the 1996 report to the United Nations Commission on Human Rights, Radhika Coomaraswamy, the United Nations Special Rapporteur on Violence against Women, clearly identified the Japanese military comfort women issue as military sexual slavery in wartime. Through the report to the UN Sub-Commission on the Promotion and Protection of Human Rights in 1998, Special Rapporteur Gay McDougall also stated that "implicit in the definition of slavery are notions concerning limitations on autonomy, freedom of movement and power to decide matters relating to one's sexual activity." Through a statement Japanese Chief Cabinet Secretary Kono Yohei made in August 1993, the Japanese government acknowledged that comfort women "lived in misery at comfort stations under a coercive atmosphere." All subsequent Japanese administrations have upheld the Kono Statement.

Arguing that comfort women cannot be defined as sex slaves because they weren't forcibly mobilized or because they received wages in some cases both goes against the definition of slavery as defined by the international law. Accusing Korea of spreading falsehoods causing comfort women to be perceived as sex slaves is a dismissal of the international discussions. It took somewhere between three decades to a century to establish the understanding that the Japanese military "comfort women" system was none other than sexual slavery.

⟨Reference 1⟩ Monument in Tribute to Comfort Women Victims

Mount Namsan, Seoul (Aug 14, 2019)
The victim Kim Hak-soon gazes at a Korean, Chinese, and Philippine girl holding hands.

In front of the Japanese embassy in Seoul (Dec 14, 2011)

Shanghai, China (Oct 22, 2016)

Glendale, California (Jul 30, 2013)

Fairfax County, Virginia (May 30, 2014)

28

Modernization from Japanese Colonial Rule?

To execute colonial rule more efficiently and publicize its achievements as a colonial ruler, the Government-General published a statistical yearbook based on the annual survey it conducted on all spheres of colonial society. Despite such motives behind the survey, a detailed analysis of the statistics it produced offers a certain degree of insight into the reality of colonial Korea. However, those who place too much faith in the statistical yearbook consider it as proof that Japanese colonial rule contributed to the development of Korean society, especially in terms of economic development. This is what scholars commonly refer to as the colonial modernization theory, but does it represent the reality of colonial Korea?

The theory is based on an array of points that explained how Japan contributed to the economic development of an extremely backward, stagnant society like Korea: ① the massive influx of Japanese capital, especially since the 1930s, coupled with Japan's political power and leadership facilitated Korea's economic development, ② which led to an increase in the per capita income of Korea, expanded its roads, railways, and industrial facilities, ③ allowed the spread of education to nurture the manpower modernization required, and ④ built the foundation for the rapid economic development Korea experienced since the 1960s.

The aforementioned points discussed through the colonial modernization theory are met with considerable criticism. While few would deny that Korea's economic, productive capacity expanded under Japanese colonial rule, many have pointed out that when approaching Joseon's development from this perspectives, Korea's reality as a colony is completely disregarded in the discussion. The major criticisms of the colonial modernization theory are as follows.

First, it is necessary to consider who took the fruit of the economic development. The lives of Koreans did gradually improve, but the ones who benefited the most from Korea's economic development were Japanese capitalists and landowners as well as a handful of Korean capitalists and landowners. Hence, the colonial modernization theory fails to consider that the reality many farmers in Korea faced from being driven out of their land and forced to migrate to Jiandao or Manchuria.

Second, a period of rapid economic development in Korea coincides with Japan's invasion of mainland China, which subsequently turned Korea into Japan's logistics base. The capital that flowed in from Japan specifically financed the munitions and heavy industry of Korea, which caused Korea to serve as a subcontractor within Japan's capitalist system.

The economic growth of Korea was therefore achieved by mobilizing people to serve at battlefields and work sites that had nothing to do with their everyday lives.

Third, infrastructure such as roads and railways were built upon a framework of exploitation. In the case of railways, the purpose of building them was clear from the beginning. Railways were meant to transport troops the way the Gyeongui Line was used during the Russo-Japanese War. They also passed through grain producing areas to be able to easily transport plundered grains and other commodities. Apart from creating markets and transporting food supplies, railways and roads were necessary for the Japanese military and police to dominate Korea. However, such infrastructure offered little benefit to the Koreans who had to pay pricey fares to enjoy convenience in transportation.

Fourth, the essence of modernization should be reexamined. The history of the West indicates that modernization brings not only socioeconomic progress, but political and cultural progress as well. In particular, political progress entails the development of democracy and the expansion of rights for individuals and women. Unfortunately, Japanese colonial rule oppressed the rights of Koreans. The increase of educational opportunities did not lead to the cultivation of citizens to serve as pillars of a modern, capitalist society. Education in Korea only aimed at cultivating obedient subjects of the Japanese emperor. Japanese imperialism had no intention of allowing autonomy, let alone suffrage.

Imperialism and colonialism emerged as capitalism developed in modern history. Imperialist states basically incorporated colonies into their own economic system by using colonies as a commodity market and a source of raw material, food, and cheap labor. Even after its liberation and division, Korea wholly inherited the industrial and regional imbalances from the colonial period. Moreover, the Korean War destroyed most of the industrial facilities built under the colonial rule. Korea's current economic status was solely achieved through the efforts of its own people.

〈Reference 1〉 Railways in 1927

Upon the outbreak of the Russo-Japanese War in 1904, the construction of the Gyeongbu and Gyeongui Lines was launched for the transportation of troops. Japan confiscated land and mobilized Koreans to accelerate the construction. The map above shows that the railway passed through major grain producing areas in the Jeolla Province.

〈Reference 2〉 Gyeongseong (Seoul) Station Under Construction

- Source: Seoul teukbyeolsisa pyeonchan wiwonhoe, *Ilje chimnyak araeseo ui Seoul* (1910-1945) [Seoul Under Japanese Aggression (1910-1945)] (Seoul: Seoul Metropolitan City, 2002), 165.

29

Individual Right to Claim Compensation: The 2018 Korean Supreme Court Ruling

The Japanese government argues that all rights to claim were settled through the 1965 Korea-Japan Claims Agreement, including the individual rights of victims of Japan's forced mobilization. On what grounds did the Korean Supreme Court dismiss Japan's argument and acknowledge the individual rights of forced mobilization victims to claim compensation?

Since the 1990s after the Cold War ended, victims of Japanese aggressions all over Asia began to sue the Japanese government and companies for compensation. Such lawsuits were filed because Japan did not compensate individuals at all while states were compensated according to the San Francisco Peace Treaty and other bilateral agreements. The number of lawsuits for individual compensation have amounted to 101 as of 2019. However, not one of them has managed to rule in favor of the victims.

After losing the lawsuits filed with Japanese courts, Korean victims of Japan's forced mobilization filed lawsuits with Korean courts. They lost the first and second trials because the Korean courts recognized the binding force of the Japanese High Court's ruling. However, the Korean Supreme Court overturned the Busan High Court's decision that was made on May 25, 2012 and remanded the case. And on October 30, 2018, the final ruling ordered compensation to be made to victims of forced labor.

The Korean Supreme Court disagreed with the Japanese court ruling, which deemed the application of the National Mobilization Law and National Conscription Ordinance to the Korean peninsula and plaintiffs (victims) as effective based on "a normative understanding that Japan's colonial rule over the Korean peninsula was legitimate." The Korean Supreme Court found that the Japanese ruling went against the core values of the Korean Constitution, which regards Japan's forced mobilization as illegal. Confirming the Japanese ruling would therefore "contradict the good customs and other social orders of the Republic of Korea."

On the key issue of whether the 1965 Claims Agreement caused the expiration of the plaintiffs' individual right to claim compensation, the Korean Supreme Court ruled that the 1965 Claims Agreement did not apply to the plaintiffs because they were exercising their right to claim compensation for damages against Japanese companies for committing inhumane, illegal acts that directly affected Japan's illegal colonial rule over the Korean peninsula.

The Korean Supreme Court regarded the 1965 Claims Agreement as means to "resolve financial and civil receivable and liability issues" between Korea and Japan based on Article 4 of the San Francisco Peace Treaty. As such, the agreement had not been meant to settle claims for compensation due to Japan's illegal colonial rule. The supreme court also highlighted the fact that the Japanese government had fundamentally denied legal compensation for forced mobilization without acknowledging the illegality of colonial rule.

The Japanese government claims that the Korean Supreme Court ruling goes against international law because individual rights to claim have already been settled through the 1965 Claims Agreement. Nevertheless, the Japanese government is aware that individual rights to claim cannot be expired through an international agreement. In a lawsuit involving several Chinese victims of forced labor filed against Nishimatsu Construction in 2007, a Japanese high court ruled that the plaintiffs retained the right to claim regardless of any international agreement.

Victims still suffering from human rights violations during Japan's illegal colonial rule must be relieved. However, Japan maintains that all rights to claim have been settled through the 1965 Claims Agreement. The victims' individual right to claim is required to rectify human rights violations. That right cannot be expired through international treaties or domestic law because such an expiration would be a violation of a person's basic rights.

The Japanese government should embrace the victim-centered approach that was unanimously adopted at a United Nations General

Assembly in 2005 and accept the Korean Supreme Court ruling on compensation for forced mobilization victims that is based on international human rights law. By doing so, they may sincerely take historical responsibility for the rehabilitation of victims and the rectification of human rights and dignity.

〈Reference 1〉 Korean Supreme Court en banc session (October 30, 2018)

- Source: *Yonhap News*.

"The court determined that there was an error in the misapprehension of the legal principle of the Japanese judgment, as the reasoning behind the final judgment of the Japanese court ("the Japanese judgment") which rejected Gap's aforementioned claim perceived that applying the National Mobilization Law to Gap et al and the Korean peninsula was effective, based on a normative understanding that Japan's colonial rule over the Korean peninsula was legitimate; however, the ROK Constitution perceives that the Japanese Occupation Period was an illegal occupation, thus any legal relationship resulting from the illegal occupation that contradicts the spirit of the Constitution is deemed ineffective; the reasoning of the Japanese judgment directly contradicts the core values of the ROK Constitution, since the ROK Constitution perceives forced mobilization itself as illegal; therefore, approving the Japanese judgment would contradict the good customs or other social orders of ROK and is therefore deemed invalid." (Korean Supreme Court Decision on May 24, 2012).

30

Waiting for a Sincere Apology

Did the Japanese government acknowledge the illegality and injustice of its colonial rule and offer an apology? It took six years after Korea's liberation before Korea and Japan were able to start negotiating the normalization of their diplomatic relations in 1951. However, negotiations were sometimes suspended due to the gap in the two countries' respective perception of the thirty-five years of Japanese colonial rule. At the second meeting of the Property Claims Committee held on October 15, 1953, the chief Japanese delegate Kubota Kanichiro remarked that "Japan built railways and ports and cleared lands for farming in Korea, and the Japanese Ministry of Finance even donated as much as twenty million Japanese Yen every year." This was criticized by the Korean Minister of Foreign Affairs Byeon Yeong-tae who said "such remarks openly disrespectful of Korea are possible because the Japanese have not yet abandoned their aggressive aspirations toward Korea." This incident caused bilateral negotiations to be suspended until the Japanese government withdrew Kubota's remark in December 1957. Japanese colonial rule was regarded as illegal in Korea, but legal in Japan. And fifteen years of negotiations failed to change the Japanese government's perception. In the end, this difference was not properly addressed, but temporarily patched up in order to normalize the two countries' diplomatic relations.

On January 17, 1965, the Japanese Foreign Minister Shiina Etsusaburo mentioned during his visit to Korea that it was "truly regrettable that there have been unfortunate times in the two countries' long history" and added that Japan was "deeply remorseful." The remark may not have been completely satisfying, but it was a sign that the Japanese government was willing to officially acknowledge the injustice of its colonial rule. Although the illegality of colonial rule is yet to be acknowledged by political leaders in Japan, they have admitted that Japanese colonial rule and wars of aggression inflicted tremendous damage and pain upon Korea and several other Asian countries.

Words of apology and remorse for causing harm through colonial rule and aggression were included in the general policy speech Prime Minister Hosokawa Morihiro gave before the Diet on August 23, 1993 and in the statement Prime Minister Murayama Tomiichi issued on August 15, 1995. All subsequent prime ministers have declared that they will uphold the Murayama statement. The statement was further developed through the Kim Dae-jung-Obuchi Keizō Declaration in 1998 and the statement Prime Minister Kan Naoto issued on August 10, 2010, stipulating Korea

〈**Reference 1**〉 Kim Dae-jung-Obuchi Keizō Declaration (1998)

In the presence of their respective minister of foreign affairs, Korean President Kim Dae-jung and Japanese Prime Minister Obuchi Keizō are signing the joint declaration for a new twenty-first century partnership in October 1998 at Akasaka Palace in Tokyo.

- Source: *Joongang Ilbo*, May 20, 2018.

as the victim of Japanese colonial rule and adding details about the damage it suffered.

This trend of acknowledgement, however, did not apply to the statement Prime Minister Abe Shinzo made on August 14, 2015. Furthermore, Prime Minister Abe has been glorifying Japanese colonial rule and wars of aggression, visiting Yasukuni Shrine to pay his respects, and denying the fact that the Japanese military comfort women were mobilized by force. An apology does not guarantee closure. What is more important than making an apology is to remain true to the words used in the apology. Prime Minister Abe's words and actions have denied the apologies for colonial rule that the Japanese government made until now. Japan's sincere apology is necessary to advance human rights and ensure peace in Northeast Asia and the rest of the world.

〈Reference 2〉 Prime Minister Kan Naoto's Statement (Aug 10, 2010)

This year marks a significant juncture for the Japan-Republic of Korea relationship. In August precisely one hundred years ago, the Japan-Korea Annexation Treaty was concluded, making the beginning of the colonial rule of thirty-six years. As demonstrated by strong resistance such as the Samil independence movement, the Korean people of that time was deprived of their country and culture, and their ethnic pride was deeply scarred by the colonial rule which was imposed against their will under the political and military circumstances.

I would like to face history with sincerity. I would like to have the courage to directly confront the facts of history and humility to accept them, as well as to be honest to reflect upon the errors of our own. Those who render pain tend to forget it while those who suffered cannot forget it easily. To the tremendous damage and sufferings that this colonial rule caused, I express here once again my feelings of deep remorse and my heartfelt apology.

History of
Japan's Intrusions
into Korea

Thirty Images and Documents on

Japan's invasion of Korea

published in November 30, 2020

Edited by Northeast Asian History Foundation
published by Northeast Asian History Foundation

Registration 312-2004-050(2004. 10. 18.)
Address 81, Tongil-ro, Seodaemun-gu, Seoul, Republic of Korea
Tel 02-2012-6065
Fax 02-2012-6189
Website www.nahf.or.kr
Printed in Chung-Ah Publishing Co.

ISBN 978-89-6187-574-5 04910
978-89-6187-482-3 (set)